Praise for *Begin Again*

"*Begin Again* is a sacred invitation to walk forward in our own lives without shame or regret. Leeana Tankersley's words stir the soul and hold space for anyone who feels stuck, overcome, or undone. I want to give this tender, powerful book to every woman in my life."

Emily P. Freeman, *Wall Street Journal* bestselling author of *Simply Tuesday*

"*Begin Again* is easily the most beautiful thing I have read all year. Profound and soulful, it is a book that will change everything you believe about releasing hurt and choosing rest. Charming and generous, Leeana is the type of writer who gives words to the things we have trouble saying out loud, and offers gentle wisdom that is both fresh and deep. A unique mixture of raw honesty and expectant hope, *Begin Again* leaves you better in every possible way. This is a book you will want to share with your friends and read multiple times."

Mandy Arioto, president and CEO of MOPS International; author of *Starry Eyed*

"*Begin Again* is inspirational, but it isn't a self-help book. It is a treasury of grace. With humor and wisdom and a poetic voice, Leeana reminds us we are not required to fix ourselves, and every day offers countless moments in which we can begin again to receive rest and renewal. Leeana filters Scripture, poetry, and ancient wisdom through the lens of the ordinary extraordinary life she and her family live in an old California house scented with jasmine and sheltered by rustling palm trees. Leeana makes room for us in this place and invites us to join her on a journey that begins again and again, yet carries us forward with each new beginning. Now I know that beginning again is not a sign of failure. We begin again because every day offers some fresh grace blowing in as if through an open window. This book is for every woman wondering how to open that window and how to keep it open."

Christie Purifoy, author of *Roots and Sky: A Journey Home in Four Seasons*

Praise for *Brazen*

"Leeana's words have taught me how to be at home with myself."

Myquillyn Smith, The Nester, author of *Cozy Minimalist Home*

"We all want to find our voice, feel comfortable in our own skin, and come out of hiding. Leeana is a trustworthy companion on this journey of becoming broken and beautiful."

Rebekah Lyons, author of *Freefall to Fly*

"If you ever feel inclined to apologize for your own existence in this world, then please, please read this insightful, soulful book. A writer with as much spice and sass as compassion and grace, Leeana is the friend providing you with peace in your personhood as she shows you how to see yourself as your Creator does. This book will both unhook you from your false press as it anchors you to your true identity: You are a brazen and beloved creation worth celebrating."

Kristen Strong, author of *Girl Meets Change: Truths to Carry You through Life's Transitions*

Praise for *Breathing Room*

"Leeana says out loud the things we all feel, and she says it with grace and eloquence. I'm so thankful for her honesty and her wisdom. Reading these pages is like sitting with a friend, and that's the best thing I can think of."

Shauna Niequist, author of *Bread & Wine*

"A new lyrical voice in a crowded world, Tankersley tells a tale of hope, reality, and everything in between."

Claire Díaz-Ortiz, author, speaker, and innovator at Twitter, Inc.

ALWAYS WE BEGIN AGAIN

ALWAYS WE BEGIN AGAIN

Stepping into the Next, New Moment

LEEANA TANKERSLEY

Revell
a division of Baker Publishing Group
Grand Rapids, Michigan

Published by Revell
a division of Baker Publishing Group
PO Box 6287, Grand Rapids, MI 49516-6287
www.revellbooks.com

Printed in the United States of America

Library of Congress Cataloging-in-Publication Data
Names: Tankersley, Leeana, 1975– author.
Title: Always we begin again : stepping into the next, new moment / Leeana Tankersley.
Description: Grand Rapids : Revell, [2019]
Identifiers: LCCN 2019007259 | ISBN 9780800737184 (cloth)
Subjects: LCSH: Christian women—Prayers and devotions. |
Encouragement—Religious aspects—Christianity—Meditations.
Classification: LCC BV4844 .T36 2019 | DDC 242/.643—dc23
LC record available at https://lccn.loc.gov/2019007259

Portions of this text are taken from *Breathing Room* (2014), *Brazen* (2016), and *Begin Again* (2018).

Author is represented by ChristopherFerebee.com, Attorney and Literary Agent.

19 20 21 22 23 24 25 7 6 5 4 3 2 1

To my mom, Melinda,

who has, my entire life, modeled the dailyness of faith and who is with me now as I begin again.

Contents

Introduction YOU MAKE THE PATH

I'll show up and take care of you
as I promised and bring you back home.
—Jeremiah 29:11

At my church, there is a stained glass in the front center of the sanctuary. I look at it every Sunday as it rises up behind the pastor's head. The stained glass is two figures—an angel and a person. The angel is holding the person and they are looking out to the horizon together, the person with her hand above her eyes as if straining to look out and see.

Most of us are looking for the path, some kind of clarity, and it's practically impossible to see at times no matter how hard we look, how hard we strain for answers. It's just not yet materializing exactly.

The most recent season of my life has been marked with significant endings and beginnings. I have been navigating the end of my marriage, which was not my desire. As a result, my three kids and I have moved across the country from bustling San Diego to a quiet town in central Virginia, which has been nourishing and also very new. And now we wait for more to be revealed.

What happens when the path is just entirely unclear? What do we do when we cannot see much of anything at all?

Where is the path, exactly? Where is the person or people I thought would be with me on the journey? Who will accompany me going forward? When will they arrive? Where are we headed, if you had to say? What am I supposed to bring with me? What am I supposed to leave behind? I get into a fit about every third day over these questions.

I recently heard these beautiful lines by Spanish poet Antonio Machado:

> Pathmaker, there is no path
> You make the path by walking
> By walking, you make the path.

I find such great comfort in these words. The path appears as we walk, one step at a time. By walking, we make the path. We step into the very next, new moment and then the next and then the next. We begin again, despite all odds.

The path does not arise or clarify because we run faster, think harder, or work more efficiently. The path arises and clarifies one grace-filled, love-filled, faith-filled step at a time. This is how we will make the entire journey.

And so we will need courage, strength, peace, resolve, patience, faith, grace for ourselves and for others . . . all the things we do not naturally come by on our own. In other words, we will need reminders of who we are and who God is.

I've collected some of the reminders I return to over and over again, the truths that have sustained me. Here they are, a collection of daily readings that I hope will companion you as you step into each new moment on your particular path.

You'll read about New Normals and Messy Middles and Soul Bullies and Come Aparts. You'll read about the wall and the Soul Voice and Warrior Sisters and being brazen. Somewhere in the midst of it all, I believe you will find what God has for you.

And, like the image in the stained glass, you will remember that even in our greatest uncertainties, we are held. It's all held.

May every word whisper to you . . .

> There is always a hand reaching toward you.
> There is always grace available.
> And there is always a chance to begin again.

Love upon love,
Leeana

day 1 THE SACREDNESS OF BEGINNINGS

Make me brave. Lead me into the enormous space of becoming.

—Sue Monk Kidd

Ten years ago, I was a brand-new mother to boy/girl twins, and everything felt enormous. My love was enormous. My fear was enormous. My self-contempt was enormous. My exhaustion, enormous. The pile of empty Diet Coke cans, enormous. The babies' beauty, enormous. The weight of how perfect it all was, just waiting for me to mess it up, enormous.

I could not cut a path through the extraordinary landscape. It was all just huge. And so I felt nailed to the couch, floating, in love and entirely anxious. Like I wanted to crawl out of my own skin. Of course, you have no idea what I'm talking about whatsoever.

It was in these very early days of motherhood that I read the line from the Rule of Saint Benedict, which transformed into not just a line but a lifeline and has been with me every day since those winter days over a decade ago:

Always we begin again.

Benedict's rule for monks called out the holiness of repetition, even the spiritual efficacy of it, though our culture preaches only the opposite. It gave a certain grace to beginnings.

Because that's all those days were: one beginning after another. And let's be honest, that's what so much of life is—learning how, and learning how again, over and over.

Each day is brand new, after all. We've never lived this day before. It is certainly difficult to not get impatient, even contemptuous, with ourselves over our utter noviceness in life. And the difficulty of being new and inexperienced tempts us to become experts, or in some cases pretend we are experts, long before we actually are.

Beginning again is permission to be unaccomplished, to be a beginner, to be brand new. More than permission too, a sense that we are right where we should be and that the beginning space is actually a holy space, not just a layover on our way to something better.

• • •

We can fall into the false belief that being a beginner is being a failure. Are you starting out at something and your newness is causing you to doubt yourself, tempting you to believe you are inadequate?

Write out the new thing or things you are navigating.

____

____

____

God, give me grace with myself as I tolerate being a beginner. Amen.

day 2 TO OPEN UP

> *Anyone or anything*
> *that does not bring you alive*
> *is too small for you.*
>
> *—David Whyte*

It was late spring and the breeze brought up the jasmine from the gate where it climbs. I walked through the house, room by room, opening doors and windows. Letting air move through the house. Every opened window, every opened door, a prayer.

Come in.
Help.
Thank you.

I opened the entire house. Cranked windows wide open. Found stools and baskets to prop the doors. And then I stood in the very center of our house. I tilted my chin up slightly, and I closed my eyes and let the air move across my face.

Sometimes a house feels tight, no matter how many square feet it is. Sometimes a heart and a life feel tight. Sometimes a marriage feels tight. Sometimes our work or our calling feels tight. Sometimes the skin we're in feels tight. We need a door or a window to open, a fresh breeze of perspective, the movement of change, but we don't always know how to get there from here.

Opening life up when things feel tight is a vulnerable move. Keeping everything sealed feels so much safer. What will we find when we open the door? What will slide in through the screen? What is waiting for us behind the windows?

When this tightness arrives—for any reason—my initial response is to lock, seal, slam, secure, bolt. I shut out. I don't want my imperfections to be witnessed. I don't think I can tolerate that kind of exposure. I do this as a means of self-protection. I do this as a way to control my image as someone who is special.

I avoided until I could no longer avoid anymore, and that's when the gentle voice whispered in my ear, like it had so many times before, *Leeana, always we begin again*.

The word *begin* has unique origins. In fact, there aren't many other words like it. In its etymology, one of the meanings of begin is "to open up."

When we need to begin, often what keeps us from beginning is our desire to shut down or slam shut in the precise place where we need to open up. We feel cornered, shamed, stuck, and so our natural tendency is to go inward.

But God is always patiently reaching toward us. And all we really have to do is reach back, but this requires us to open up. Opening up is vulnerable. Letting others in, letting air and space and light in, letting God in, letting truth in . . . feels like we're inviting exposure. And, I guess we are. But usually uncovering and opening is what it's going to take to get us out of the corner we're in.

I know it feels counterintuitive . . . to let the light shine on something we'd prefer to keep hidden, to reach out when we'd rather turn in, to actually believe that the truth—however scary—will be what sets us free. Can we trust that opening up has more gifts than staying shut, hiding, defending?

Is there a place in your life where you are slammed shut? A relationship, a fear, an issue of faith? A place where you cannot let God in, cannot let others in? Is God inviting you to open up?

Remember:

> There is always a hand reaching toward you.
> There is always grace available.
> There is always a chance to begin again.

. . .

Imagine yourself holding on to something, hovered over it, protecting it, but it's all you can see. You cannot see the world, the beauty, the possibility beyond you because you are focused on what you're holding. Imagine God is reaching toward you, asking you to open up, let him see what you are holding.

What is God saying to you?

____

____

____

What do you say back to God?

day 3 HERE, GOD

I have held many things in my hands, and I have lost them all; but whatever I have placed in God's hands, that I still possess.

—Martin Luther

I always thought of surrendering as giving up. But I spent some time with the word over the last year, and as I looked into the etymology of *surrender*, I found that one of the meanings is "to give back." When things aren't working in our lives—a relationship, a plan, a dream, a desire—one of the most important things we can do is surrender it. And it's the hardest.

As long as we have our grubby mitts on the person or the pursuit, that's where it will stay, in our hands. But when we surrender our deepest needs and longings to God, we don't give up, we give them back to him. We say, *Here, God, you can do so much more with this than I can. I'm squeezing the life out of this person or this plan, and I need you to take it from me and do what you will with it. I'm giving it back to you.*

This is how we move forward instead of staying stuck. If you're in a closed, frustrating loop of behavior or thinking, say a prayer of surrender to God, giving back the thing you desperately want to clutch on to.

And then do it again and again and again. A hundred times in one day if you have to. *God, I surrender this dream. God, I surrender this longing. God, I surrender this goal. Infuse it with your love and grace. I trust you entirely.*

What is one thing in your life you need
to surrender to God in prayer?

Here, God, I'm finally giving you . . .

day 4 TENDING

True to your word,
you let me catch my breath
and send me in the right direction.
—Psalm 23:3

When we're locked up, anxious, overwhelmed, restless, it's so difficult to do the small acts of each day. At least it is for me. Washing my face, watering the plants, folding laundry, chopping veggies for dinner . . . all feel impossible. I want shortcuts, and I want to be done with things once and for all.

Tending—the act of giving attention to someone or something—is an ongoing endeavor. Tending requires us to begin again and again by its very nature. Because it requires participation and even discipline, tending is good for us. It teaches us to reinvest, to get our hands back into our own lives, to care for something small or menial as an act of love and health.

Tending helps tether us to today.

If you are swirling today, trying to figure out what big step you need to take next in your life, try to start small instead. Tend to something: drink water, take a walk, pull weeds or cut dead branches off your trees, fold a load of laundry, chop veggies, stir soup. Pay attention to your hands as they move. Tending helps tether us to today. It makes us slow down and participate in the menial and the mundane.

When I am hustling and striving and trying to hold things together, tending is one of the last things on my list, *because it requires me to let the moment fall open.* And I feel I just don't have the strength to let that happen.

Tend. Attend. Be in attendance. Present and accounted for.

As I bring my worries and fears and control to God and give them back to him, tending feels more possible. And more than that, I feel drawn—by the Soul Voice—to the raised bed in the yard, the brush and my daughter Lane's wild mane, the prep for the chimichurri sauce, the potted bougainvillea. The voice in my soul invites me to the lemon tree, to tie my turquoise tennis shoes and walk the rolling hills, to read just one selection from the poetry anthology.

This is just unreal, if you ask me, because tending does not yield accomplishment. It's just a practice.

• • •

Is there something you feel drawn to tending right now?

Today, I want to take care of . . .

day 5 HELD, NO MATTER WHAT

Christ with me,
Christ before me,
Christ behind me,
Christ in me,
Christ beneath me,
Christ above me,
Christ on my right,
Christ on my left.
—St. Patrick

Do you know that no matter what, you are held? Mysteriously and benevolently, you are held. Your job is to give in to this held-ness instead of trying to squirm away so you can go prove how worthy you are.

You are held. For no other reason than love. Wild, right? I love these words from Exodus 14:14:

> The LORD will fight for you; you need only to be still. (NIV)

But sometimes being right where we are is the hardest work. Sometimes it takes more energy and discipline to "be still" than to spring into frantic action. That's why it's so important for us to meditate on the truth that God's got us, he's holding things together that we couldn't possibly fix or control, he's conspiring on our behalf. I know it's never easy to let go and fall back into God's love, but that's what we've got to do.

God is beside, before, behind, and beneath us. We sink back into God's great love and provision and we choose rest instead of relentless trying. *Thank you, God, that it's never all up to me. Please help me to be still today, to sink back into your love and embrace. Amen.*

If I can sit in this truth, that I am held by Love no matter what, I can and will begin again. This is what you are to take with you today. No big plan. Just the simple yet profound knowledge of your held-ness. No matter what, God is holding you.

He says, *You do not need to do more, fix yourself, or hold anything together. You just need to fall back into my grace, trade your trying for trust. Where you are broken and bruised is exactly the place, not in spite of that place, that I want to show you you're beautiful.*

• • •

Imagine yourself, your life, your circumstances, all held by benevolent hands. What does it feel like to let go, fall back, let down? What scares you? What relieves you?

God, it's hard for me to be still because . . .

____

____

____

day 6 LED BY LISTENING

But God *wasn't to be found in the wind; after the wind an earthquake, but* God *wasn't in the earthquake; and after the earthquake fire, but* God *wasn't in the fire; and after the fire a gentle and quiet whisper.*

—1 Kings 19:12

I don't need to tell you that the world is a noisy place. And if you're anything like me, your mind and your body are also noisy places to inhabit, sometimes pulling you in so many different directions that you end up paralyzed.

Noise fragments. It distracts and numbs, making us unable to hear God's voice or even our own Soul Voices. And, to some extent, noise is unavoidable. So we have to find ways to counterbalance the disintegrating distractions that are all around us.

For me, the practice of listening has helped me cut through all the competing messages and turn my ear to my own thoughts and feelings as well as the still small whisper of Love. Listening is a discipline. The root of the word *listen* means "to honor," and you have to make time to honor something in your life. But here's all it takes:

Carve out five to ten minutes and find a quiet space. Write at the top of a piece of paper: *God, what do you want to say to me today?*

And then listen. If interrupting thoughts break in—like your grocery list or a phone call you need to make—no problem. Dedicate a box at the top right of your paper for anything you need to jot down that's unrelated to your listening.

Write down what you hear from God. Write down what you want to say back to him—questions, concerns, frustrations, gratitude—anything. Just sit and listen to him and to yourself and record your dialogue. It's OK if it goes poorly at first. It's OK if you feel distracted or annoyed or frantic or itchy. All of these things are likely. Just keep your butt in the chair.

"Listening is something you never regret," I recently heard acoustic ecologist Gordon Hempton say.

I think that's true. And with more voices than ever bombarding us, vying for our attention and soul space, we could just as easily grab for a solution in the din. That would be quicker. Ingest some information.

But I think most of us know deep down that the noise is not where we will find our guidance. We are led by listening.

Listening is about trading our trying for trust. This is how we find true rest, I believe. Listening is a begin-again kind of ritual. It's never finished and it's always possible, and it's waiting to give us living and breathing gifts that are new every morning.

• • •

God, what do you want to say to me today?

____

____

____

day 7 BELIEVE, DON'T BULLY

It's as if there's a part of you that so rails against being shattered by love that you shatter yourself first.

—Geneen Roth

Sure you can get results by punishment, shaming, bullying. Of course you can. That's why these tactics are used in homes, workplaces, teams, and the schoolyard. You can manipulate people using force, but that doesn't mean you will ultimately produce transformation.

We often approach ourselves with the belief that if we can just punish, bully, belittle, or deprive ourselves enough, we will ultimately get the results we are after. But I am starting to think we make lasting changes in our lives when we believe we deserve more, we believe we are capable of something greater, we believe we were made for wholeness, we decide to protect the God-image inside us.

Yes, you can push and prod yourself into action. But I promise you it will not last. You will be living out of scarcity instead of abundance. And abundance—spaciousness—is where you will thrive.

Is there an area of your life where you are trying to bully yourself into action or results? Instead of focusing on how bad you are, how much you've failed, focus on the reasons why you deserve to pursue health and wholeness in your life. Focus on your values, your gifts you want to give the world, your dignity as a human being, and the image of God in you.

• • •

How are you bullying yourself—either through thoughts, self-talk, or actions? Make a list.

God, who do you say I am?

You are . . .

day 8 EVERY WALL IS A DOOR

We'll know we've been raised from the dead
when everything becomes a door—
every brick wall,
every dead end . . .

—Father Francis Dorff

Somewhere in your life, you are experiencing a wall. You have done everything in your power to change this, read all the advice, tried all the strategies, pooled all the collective wisdom, and here you are at the wall. Maybe the wall is an ending, a failure, a nothing-is-ever-going-to-change situation, burnout, an illness, a rejection.

For many of us, we experience the wall when all our normal ways of coping just aren't delivering anymore. Our strategies, denial, numbing aren't producing, aren't keeping us going, like they once did. And we no longer have the strength or stamina or even desire to push through.

When we hit the wall, we can do a number of things. We can act like it's not happening (denial) and bang our heads against it or walk away as if the hard thing isn't even there. We can go sideways (destruction) and blow up our lives. This happens regularly. The pain and the tension of the wall cause us to just lose it.

Or, we can see the entire wall-hitting as something completely different: a grace. Could the wall possibly be a door leading to something sacred—some kind of new life, transformation, revelation, truth, freedom—that you never could have experienced without the wall? And could you open that door and see what God might have for you on the other side?

• • •

Are you hitting a wall of some kind? Name the wall below. How might the wall be a door? And what might the door be leading you to or toward?

day 9 BURN IT DOWN

> *I want to unfold.*
> *Let no place in me hold itself closed,*
> *for where I am closed, I am false.*
>
> —*Rainer Maria Rilke*

What are you serving that is no longer serving you? That's a question I've been considering lately. What's something in my life that I am (over)committed to, pouring energy into, that isn't offering me anything productive in return?

We assume that some of our habits or strategies are keeping us safe, insulated, happy, when really they are secretly keeping us silenced and small.

Recently, a phrase kept echoing through me, like a persistent whisper. It was this: "Burn it down." I had no idea what that phrase meant or why it was coming to me, but I committed to listening. And as I paid attention, I realized that I would hear "Burn it down" whenever I was trying to please someone else or win them over, whenever I was trying to cover over someone else's bad behavior, whenever I was trying to keep the peace at all costs. "Burn it down, Leeana. Burn it down."

I was truly invested in patterns and behaviors that were doing nothing for me. I thought they were helping, but they were only, ultimately, hurting. I am learning that it's OK to let go of false promises of safety and security, even though it's so dang hard. We cannot hold on to all our old ways and trust God for new life at the same time.

• • •

Is there something God is inviting you to burn down? A behavior, a pattern, a way of thinking, a way of being in your relationships? What is the cost to burning it down?

God, help me burn down my . . .

day 10 ACKNOWLEDGE THE AGITATION

The purpose of life is not to maintain personal comfort;
it's to grow the soul.

—*Christina Baldwin*

Usually the agitation in our lives is trying to tell us something. Or rather, God is trying to tell us something through the agitation. I believe—even though I really don't like it—that the invitation is in the agitation. If you want to discern the work God wants you to do in your life, look at the tension.

I know, I know. This is the last place we want to look. We want to ignore the rub; it feels dumb, if not dangerous, to turn toward it. *If I don't look that way, maybe it will all just go away.* But I've found in my own life, this agitation typically doesn't go away. We just get better at numbing it.

I believe—even though I really don't like it—that the invitation is in the agitation.

I saw a counselor last year and she told me that every time I felt overcome by obsessive thoughts it meant there was something I needed to grieve. The anxious loops of thinking were a cue that I had not grieved something important.

So instead of getting frustrated with myself when I couldn't control my thoughts, I would remind myself that the agitation was an invitation to ask myself, What do I need to grieve? It was hard work, but slowly, over time, the anxious, obsessive messages began to be less intense and when they did flare up, I knew how to sit with myself instead of run for the hills.

Certainly we cannot sit in a state of agitation at all times, but take some time today or this week and purposefully turn toward a place of discomfort, tension, or friction in your life. Be sure you are in a safe place as you do this. Where is there conflict you do not want to acknowledge? Where is there a sense of incongruence you want to ignore?

You don't have to solve anything, fix anything, or get a plan together. Simply tell God you are willing to look at these tight spaces. You are willing to acknowledge they exist. You are willing to let him speak to you.

• • •

What part of yourself or your story do you need to honor instead of ignore?

God, what are you trying to tell me through this agitation?

day 11 LOVE IS A BATTLE CRY

Watch what God does, and then you do it, like children who learn proper behavior from their parents. Mostly what God does is love you. Keep company with him and learn a life of love. Observe how Christ loved us. His love was not cautious but extravagant. He didn't love in order to get something from us but to give everything of himself to us. Love like that.

—Ephesians 5:1–2

When it comes to our transformation, God's wrath is not the fuel. God's love is the fuel. God is not a divine bully. He is a nurturing, protective mother and father. God so loved the world that he sent us a way out of our own closed loops of striving and trying. He sent us a new way: his grace. All of it, all of it, was motivated by love.

Love propels us. Love moves us. Love changes us. Love opens us up. Love offers hope. Love carries us. Love coaxes us into the next moment. Love is what helps us begin again.

"The greatest of these is love," Scripture says. This isn't a nice sentiment. This is a battle cry. Love can do things that judgment and punishment never could.

Read these words about love from 1 Corinthians 13:

> Love never gives up.
> Love cares more for others than for self.

Love doesn't want what it doesn't have.
Love doesn't strut,
Doesn't have a swelled head,
Doesn't force itself on others,
Isn't always "me first,"
Doesn't fly off the handle,
Doesn't keep score of the sins of others,
Doesn't revel when others grovel,
Takes pleasure in the flowering of truth,
Puts up with anything,
Trusts God always,
Always looks for the best,
Never looks back,
But keeps going to the end.

Love never dies.

. . .

The above passage describes God's perfect love for you.
Which line stands out to you as the kind of love you need and desire?

___

___

___

day 12 PULL UP A CHAIR

With an eye made quiet . . . we see into the life of things.
—William Wordsworth

Sit down at the table and pull up an empty chair right next to you. Invite the part of yourself that is scared, stuck, agitated, restless, perhaps young, embarrassed, obsessive, hypercontrolling—whatever part of you is feeling unwieldy—to sit down next to you. Sit her down and listen to what she has to say. Ignoring her only makes her yell louder. She needs attention. She needs to be tended to. That's what she's trying to tell you. So let her talk.

Stay with yourself. I know you want to run away from every vulnerable part of you. I know you want to silence the cry, reject the indecision, ignore the fear. But stay with yourself. The very best you can. Be where your feet are. Stop running. And stay. Imperfectly. Impatiently. Impossibly. Because she needs you.

What words does she have for you? What experiences, fears, feelings does she need you to hear? Write them down for her if needed. Be as gentle as possible with her, like you would a hurting friend, or a crying child, or a wounded puppy. Listen. Tell her that you love her and that you understand why she's feeling what she's feeling.

Of course, you might say. *Of course you feel that way.* And then gently and firmly remind her that she is loved, cherished, and welcomed, but she will not get to be in charge. The youngest, most fragile parts of you cannot make the adult decisions, cannot call all the shots.

What I've found is that the more you tend to her, the calmer and quieter she becomes. And, conversely, the more you reject her, ignore her, shame her, the louder she becomes. So anytime you feel that unwieldy part of you taking over, it's just a signal that she needs to talk to you, she needs some comfort. Pull up a chair, sit her down, listen to her, and then let her know that God will never leave her. She is known, seen, and loved . . . always.

• • •

What is the unwieldy part of you saying?

What do you want to say back to her?

____

____

____

____

____

day 13 COMMEMORATE

Let love and faithfulness never leave you;
bind them around your neck,
write them on the tablet of your heart.
—Proverbs 3:3 NIV

Some days we will see the light, we will move toward it, and we will experience the great comfort and triumph of beginning again. Nothing was perfect; it wasn't flawless by any means, but we sensed God reaching toward us, and we were able to take his hand and move into the next, new moment. We decided we didn't have to stay stuck. (Hooray!)

But if we're not careful, we'll just let the tide of life sweep us up and away, and we'll forget what just happened. We'll forget our moment of clarity and how good it felt to come out of our corner. We'll move on without giving the moment proper attention.

So I do something that helps me remember. I commemorate the clarity when it comes, even if that's rarely. To commemorate is to remember, to memorialize, to celebrate, and there are all kinds of ways we can do this.

Some people get a tattoo, some people keep a journal, some people repaint their bedroom. Because I am a writer, I get to write down and share a lot of my moments of clarity, especially when they were hard-won. But I've also started wearing my memorials too.

I have a simple rose gold necklace with the word *brazen* on it (meaning "unashamed" and "unapologetic"), and I have a beautiful bracelet my sister gave me that says *begin again* on it. I also wear the medal of St. Benedict most days. He is the father of the beautiful sentence "Always we begin again," and his presence around my neck reminds me that a next-right-step is always possible.

Commemorating helps us remember when all the condemning forces in this world would rather we forget.

• • •

Was there a moment in this last week when you were able to begin again? If so, what was the moment, and how will you remember it?

day 14 THE MESSY MIDDLE

A certain darkness is needed to see the stars.

—Osho

Are you in a Messy Middle? You know, one of those protracted, unresolved, uncertain seasons of life. You are not at the beginning, but you are nowhere near closure either. And the middle stretches on indefinitely. It tries your stamina, your faith, your belief in yourself (and maybe all of humanity), and all you want to do is hold your breath until it's all over.

I'm learning that it's precisely there in the Messy Middle that we need the brave practice of beginning again.

I think we assume that life will begin again when we are out of the Messy Middle. I know I do. "Once *this* is resolved, then I can go on living," I secretly say to myself. But I'm learning that it's precisely there in the Messy Middle that we need the brave practice of beginning again—reinvesting in the present moment, over and over again, even though it's not easy.

I am currently navigating a Messy Middle in my own life, one I never saw coming, and one I don't see the end of yet. Someone has suggested to me that perhaps most of life is a Messy Middle. I don't want to hear that or believe it. But it's likely true.

Life rarely finds that elusive equilibrium we're all waiting for. We have to do the living in the midst of the mess. So I am grateful—now more than ever, here in this Messy Middle—for the grace of beginning again, which reminds me that his mercies are new every morning, he is faithful, and he is always, always reaching toward me.

Whatever Messy Middle you're in today, I understand the urgent temptation to push through the process, grasp for control and certainty, and resist the invitation (maybe even the mandate) to be still. It doesn't matter if the Messy Middle is financial or relational or professional or physical, the interminable-ness is exhausting and makes us edgy.

So here's what's helping me:

- Taking life in 12-hour increments.
- Welcoming all the crazy feelings. I cannot say enough about this. Instead of driving away all my frantic thoughts and insane solutions, instead of judging myself for being so out of control and adolescent, I make a point to welcome it all. That doesn't mean I act on any of it. I just acknowledge all the ways that I want to jump forward, which seems to relieve some of the pressure.
- Resisting the urge to make anything urgent. So much of what I think must be decided and figured out, doesn't. It needs to unfold.
- Remembering to be good to myself, like I would a friend. Understanding. Empathetic. Patient.

- Beginning again. If I get too far ahead of myself, I recommit to the present. This moment. Now. Over and over again. This is what it means to give myself grace.

Our Messy Middles don't define us. And maybe if we can remember that truth, we can hang in a bit longer, commit to being still for another three seconds. And then another. And then another.

Grace to us as we walk in the darkness and trust that God holds us, guides us, loves us, sees us. Amen.

• • •

What Messy Middle are you currently navigating?

Once ______________________________ is resolved, then I can go on living.

____

____

____

____

____

____

day 15 SUBMIT TO SUPPORT

> *If you are sincere . . . you should not know how to proceed at times. You should not know how to get from here to there. And that puts you into a proper relationship with the world. Why? Because you have to ask for help.*
>
> —*David Whyte*

Because beginning again is a practice, a spiritual discipline, a ritual, it's the kind of thing that we usually can't sustain alone. We will need the help and support of a loving crew when we deplete our own resolve, energy, and courage.

Support comes in all kinds of packages—loving and funny friends, wise and licensed guides, sacred words, vital gatherings of like-minded people. The key is that we are willing to submit ourselves to a community of support. This does not mean we are weak or insufficient. It just means we're human, created to live in community, connected to others. Isolation kills. It really does. But hooking in to a circle of love and trust will keep us going even when we don't have the nerve anymore.

I love the picture from Scripture of the four friends carrying their invalid friend to Jesus so that he might be healed. As the story goes, the house where Jesus was teaching and healing was overrun with people, and so the four friends hoisted their friend's stretcher up to the roof and cut a hole through which they lowered him down to Jesus. So clever.

Here's what I know: It's amazing to get to be one of those people who is on the four corners of the stretcher—resourceful, strong, able, heroic. It is far less fun to be the guy on the stretcher—dependent, affected, vulnerable, incapacitated. No thanks. But, and I hate saying this, we often learn more through our vulnerabilities than we do through our capacities. And it is only through accepting the help and support of others that we are truly healed.

• • •

What support or help do you need to accept today?

What will it require for you to accept what you need?

____

____

____

____

____

____

____

day 16 NOT TODAY, SOUL BULLIES. NOT TODAY.

Therefore, there is now no condemnation for those who are in Christ Jesus, because through Christ Jesus the law of the Spirit who gives life has set you free from the law of sin and death.

—Romans 8:1–2 NIV

You will have every good intention. You will be armed with resolve and hope and new knowledge, and all you have to do is wake up, and the Soul Bullies will be on to you. They want to paralyze, shame, suffocate, embarrass, and silence you. It's just what they do. But we cannot let them have the last word about us. We cannot.

They want you to believe it's over, you're done for, things have come to a dead end. But as we considered earlier, sometimes walls are doors, and so even if you are facing what appears to be an ending, there might be some redemptive new life waiting beyond this death. We serve a different narrative than the Soul Bullies. Theirs is scarcity and either/or and punishing to get results.

Our narrative is unexpectedly abundant, wildly gracious, and it seems to seek out and serve the underdog tirelessly. So we're right at home, right in the pocket, as they say. We're where we should be: human beings on the receiving end of love and grace.

The Soul Bullies will likely never fully go away, but we have the power to put them in their place. So even if those accusing voices are creeping in and their paralyzing tactics are on the move, you can say, "Not today, Soul Bullies. Not today." And you can begin again. By the grace of God, there is now no condemnation for you, and you can begin again.

• • •

What is something The Soul Bullies are whispering in your ear? Is this the ultimate truth about you? What does God want to say to you about the Soul Bullies' words?

____

____

____

____

____

____

____

day 17 RESTLESS

Our heart is restless until it finds its rest in thee.
—St. Augustine

We are a restless breed, we human beings. We spend a lot of restless energy hurling ourselves back into an unchangeable past or forward into an unknowable future. Our Hard and our Hurts propel us and paralyze us, and it's a real trick to recommit to each moment.

We want rest. In fact, I think most of us are borderline desperate for rest: a break from all the restlessness that enervates our bodies and our minds. We want the capacity to stay right where we are instead of reeling from regret or forecasting. We want peace from the inside out, building a life on something settled and centered inside us, but all this is hard to come by, isn't it?

Which is why I believe the practice of beginning again is one of the single most significant gifts you can give yourself. Beginning again helps us live moment to moment, all the while nudging us, gently, on our journey of transformation. Without it, we get stuck. Beginning again invites us out of all the various corners we'd prefer to stay in: safety, swirling, shame, striving, scarcity, shoulds . . . to name a few.

I'm just now learning to bring my hurt to God and, in its place, receive rest. God's story is a narrative of emancipation. Here's the heart of it:

What we thought was an ending may very well be a beginning. When the hissing in our ear tells us it's over, God whispers an opportunity. Here's a place we could start from, he says. Here's a rock bottom. Let's see this for what it is: a possibility.

And we get the gift of being able to seek resurrection instead of annihilation, even though things might feel so very bleak. How is it possible that this is the start of freedom? I don't know, exactly. But I believe it could be.

Whether you are restless because of past events, future fears, or a Messy Middle; whether your life feels impossibly small or overwhelmingly enormous, here is something you can always do:

Breathe and begin again.

• • •

God, Today I am restless because . . .

day 18 UNLESS A GRAIN OF WHEAT IS BURIED

In this high place
it is as simple as this,
Leave everything you know behind.
—David Whyte

One of the most genuinely inconvenient truths I know is that often something has to die in order for something new to live. And so when we know—deep down—that something isn't working, there's also a part of us that knows what it's going to take to make the thing work again. Likely, it's going to take a death.

Those possible deaths we don't want to face, those ways of being that we're so invested in that we are gripping them with every bit of energy we can muster, lead us to thoughts like these: Don't touch my addiction to work. Don't touch my overeating. Don't look twice at my spending. Do not get close to my resentment.

Don't even think about asking me to give up my victim status. Do not, I repeat, do not, come near my codependence.

Who in their right mind wants to look death in the eyes? Or at least the possibility of death. It's hard to think about letting something fall apart, only to put it back together again in a different way.

Yet Jesus himself taught this to his people. He said,

> Listen carefully: Unless a grain of wheat is buried in the ground, dead to the world, it is never any more than a grain of wheat. But if it is buried, it sprouts and reproduces itself many times over. In the same way, anyone who holds on to life just as it is destroys that life. But if you let it go, reckless in your love, you'll have it forever, real and eternal. (John 12:24–25)

On the other side of death, the other side of surrender, is this: movement, or at least the space for movement, in the places where things have been locked down, shut down, deeply tight. We can unseal our hearts. Even just a willingness to reach for the window handle and turn it slowly. Feel the cross breeze.

In that allowing, we step into a place that is not yet. Maybe reluctantly. Maybe with the hardest of hearts, but we leave space for the possibility that something fluid and alive is on its way.

• • •

What are you keeping alive that God is inviting you to bury?

day 19 NEW LIFE STARTS IN THE DARK

I'm anticipating getting ahead of the day, instead of running to catch up with it.
I'm anticipating the way it feels to start the day with a practice instead of a panic.

—*from* Begin Again

I've started getting up at 5:00 a.m. Not every day, but more days than not. This is an anomaly for me. Normally, I am addicted to sleep. But this pre-twilight pocket, between night and morning, seems like it has something for me. "New life starts in the dark," author Barbara Brown Taylor writes. "Whether it is a seed in the ground, a baby in the womb, or Jesus in the tomb, it starts in the dark."[1]

I have a hunch this is true.

So I get up in the darkness, climb the three steps out of my bedroom, pass through the dining room, and turn on the heat as I walk by the thermostat. I walk directly to the coffee pot (obviously) and brew ten cups of coffee. And then I walk to my desk. I have a stack of books and a legal pad next to my laptop on my desk, and everything gets moved over to the kitchen table while I wait for the coffee to brew. There, at the kitchen table, I assemble my nest.

I don't know why I don't just sit down at my desk. I never do. I always walk to the kitchen table, which sits in a nook at the east end of our kitchen. My subconscious mind has not yet been interrupted. Nothing has intruded on my senses. Out the windows is only stillness.

I sit and drink black coffee and listen and write. Undistracted. I write on the top of my paper,

God, what do you want to say to me this morning?

And I just listen, keeping track of a dialogue that sometimes arrives quickly and completely and sometimes arrives fragmented and unresolved. I have been asking God this question for a while now, but never in the dark, never early in the morning like this. I'm beginning to believe, though, that there are treasures hidden in the darkness. And when you are beginning a journey of opening up, you need these hidden treasures along the way.

So if you are in the dark—literally or figuratively—pay attention. New life might just be on the way.

• • •

God, I feel like I'm in the dark about . . .

____

____

____

day 20 WAITING FOR FARAWAY THINGS

You can't force these things.
They only come about through my Spirit.
—Zechariah 4:6

Sometimes we don't have access to the answers within ourselves. They are there. I believe that. But we just can't get to them. The truth is buried or silenced and we need help to know the next right step.

The poet Rainer Maria Rilke talks about "waiting for faraway things," the mystery of holding space for something to arrive that we cannot control. Sometimes we're waiting on a miracle. A word. A whisper. Waiting for the next step to reveal itself. Waiting for a sign. A handle. A hint. For healing. Waiting for peace. Waiting for God to give us this day our daily breadcrumb. Waiting for a yes. Waiting for a no. Waiting for any answer.

I am waiting for some answers: Where will my kids and I be living next year? How will finances work out? Should I take on more work? How will all of these transitions affect my kids long term?

Rilke's emphasis on this waiting is that it's frustrating. (No kidding.) It's frustrating to be patient—with God, with ourselves, with the process—and wait for the mysterious unfolding. Waiting on something Other is not easy work. But we cannot force these things, as the prophets and the monks and the mystics all tell us.

We aren't the ones in control.

We tried that, being in control, and here we are, listening in the dark.

Most of life is an unfolding. We can create premature solutions for our lives, but I have learned that this is a dead end. What is far more effective, and far more faith-filled, is to allow the unfolding to occur. We name our desires and we hold them up to God and ask him to do what only he can do.

• • •

God, please give me grace while I'm waiting for . . .

____

____

____

day 21 SCARED-SACRED

It's rebellious to show up as a whole person.

—Courtney Martin

Parker Palmer writes,

> I pay a steep price when I live a divided life, feeling fraudulent, anxious about being found out, and depressed by the fact that I am denying my own selfhood.[1]

We all know this feeling. We are protecting someone or something, likely ourselves. We are holding on to a half-truth and basing our whole lives on it. This works for some time, but the cracks begin to show, the façade begins to break down, our soul knows it's being ignored and abandoned.

It is scary to look the contradictions in our lives right in the eye. What we say we believe but don't practice. What we expect of others but do not expect of ourselves. What we are willing to excuse away and avoid.

I am deeply longing for an undivided, honest life. One that is free from image maintenance and façading.

I am deeply longing for an undivided, honest life. One that is free from image maintenance and façading. One that doesn't require covering up and explaining away. And I don't just want to be honest with everyone else. I'm longing to be honest with myself. And I am also aware that I have to surrender in order to let God heal the divisions.

I've been too scared to do this, previously. Now, I am ready. I try to remind myself that the words *scared* and *sacred* are practically identical on first glance. Could the very fact that I'm scared be an indication I'm on sacred ground?

...

Is there an invitation in your life that scares you?

Is it possible that you are on sacred ground?

____

____

____

____

____

day 22 LET *ME* WRITE THIS STORY

I know what I'm doing. I have it all planned out—plans to take care of you, not abandon you, plans to give you the future you hope for.

—Jeremiah 29:11

God whispers to me as I lie down for the night, *Let me write this story*. I've been wrestling with him for days. I don't want to get ahead of him but he is leaving me no choice. Everything seems unclear and so I want to slyly and subtly take some control. I doubt he'll even notice. He might even bless my efforts, right?

But I can feel the dis-ease in my spirit. The nudge that says, Don't do it. It's not worth it. It won't produce what you really want. And yet I don't know how to tolerate the churning inside of me.

I have so many questions about my future. And I told God in church a couple days ago that if he wants me to keep my grabby hands off my own life then he is going to have to help me tolerate the runaway train that is my mind, the swirling and solving I can't control in my own strength.

Is there a story in your life that you are trying to write? You are trying to turn the narrative or resolve the plot? You are trying to control the characters or manipulate the setting? Is there a story in your life that you'd like to author, and God is asking you—gently, quietly—for that role?

I want to take control of certain areas of my life, create opportunities, wedge my will into the unfolding. God will let me do it. I have free will. He will let me choke and manhandle my life.

But as I put my head down on my pillow last night, he whispered, *Let me write this story*. And I knew, immediately, that this was the better way. The narrow way, the trusting way, the surrendered way, the way of relinquishment, to be sure. But also, the better way.

Some—not all—of the churning quieted. Perspective returned. Sometimes God is asking us to *move, move, move*. But most often, for me anyway, God is telling me to *breathe, breathe, breathe*. He's saying, *Let me write this story. (I promise it will turn out better than you can imagine.)*

• • •

What story are you trying to write that God may be asking you to let him create?

____

____

____

____

____

day 23 YOUR BODY KNOWS

Because the woman I love lives inside of you . . .

—Hafiz

I sit at the kitchen table and spend fifteen seconds with my eyes closed, scanning my body for tension.

Starting at the tip-top of my head and moving down my body all the way to the soles of my feet, I search for tension. You would be surprised how unaware you are of pain in your body until you take the time to acknowledge it.

First, I realize my shoulders are, like, up to my ears. Poised and ready for fight or flight. When I drop them and breathe into them, I feel how my neck, shoulders, and back are all burning. Tight, tense, overtaxed. I try to take deep breaths into that tightness, expanding the areas that are collapsed and rigid. And it hurts. It actually physically hurts.

Isn't this fascinating? Our bodies know. They are holding the story—the story of working so hard to hold it all together, of carrying the burden of making everything happen, of constructing a no-cracks façade to our work, marriages, families, homes, meals, outfits, health, bodies. At least that's what we think we're doing. We are heaping the burden of "everything is fine" on ourselves. And in this attempt to keep it all together, we are actually preventing the thing that needs to happen most: the falling apart. The opening up.

Could you get very still, breathe slowly and deeply, and let your body tell you what it needs to tell you? Do you worry that if you did this, you would collapse from all you're trying to keep managed and propped up? Could this be all the more reason to get as still as you can stand to be—even for three minutes—and check in with your body?

Re-member. That's what we're doing. We're refusing to walk around dismembered from our bodies. We believe we are whole, made in the image of God, and that our bodies are not simply a liability we must push past.

We acknowledge we are stiff and sore and in pain and we pray this important prayer: *God, help me hear what my body needs, and give me the grace to honor and provide for this beautiful body that I'd rather ignore. Help me see where I might create margin in my life and my schedule to tend to my body more regularly. Amen.*

• • •

If you get very quiet, is there an area of your body that feels sore or tight?

____

____

____

day 24 A REAL RELIEF

We feel over-responsible for everyone else and under-responsible for ourselves.

—*from* Brazen

I recently spoke at a women's event. I talked about creating breathing room during the busy holiday bustle and happened to mention that one of the ways these women could honor themselves this season was by listening to their bodies a bit more intuitively—sleep when they need to sleep, eat when they need to eat, pee when they need to pee, and so on.

I had a line of women waiting to talk to me afterward. Do you know what they all wanted to discuss? They all wanted to tell me how they constantly dance around their lives—one more load of laundry, one more lunch packed, one more email, one more meeting—because they have to pee. And it's making them frantic.

Do you know what men do when they have to pee? They walk down the hall to the bathroom. Do you know what I and so many of my friends do when we have to pee? We hold it. Until we're in pain and panicked. We are crazy people. Even animals don't do this.

Maybe it seems like a small thing, but we get in the habit of overriding our bodies and what they're trying to tell us, and I don't think it's helpful. We are believing the Soul Bullies' lie, "There is no time for me to have needs."

So, one more load of laundry. One more text message. One more sweep through the house for the flotsam and jetsam that spontaneously reproduce when I turn my head. One more item jotted in my planner. One more thing. One more thing. Just one more thing.

It takes me almost having an accident right there on the kitchen floor to decide there must be a better way. I decide to do something absolutely radical. Subversive, even. I decide I will go pee when I have to pee. I will remind myself with every trip to the bathroom that I am not superhuman. I am not God. I am not infinite in what I can hold.

And wouldn't you know? It's a real relief.

• • •

Why don't I stop and take care of myself when I have needs?

____

____

____

____

____

day 25 SABBATH = TO STOP

stop believing
in
what hurts you
—nayyirah
waheed

Did you know the word *Sabbath* translates "to stop"? Sometimes beginning again is actually about stopping instead of starting.

Where there is pretending, stop.
Where there is overcompensating, stop.
Where there is denial, stop.
Where there is avoidance, stop.
Where there are excuses, stop.

Stop the very behavior that got you here, if "here" is not working any longer. Take a Sabbath from the convincing. Just sit and feel the agitation. Today, on this Sabbath, it is not your job to fix anything.

Today, on this Sabbath, it is not your job to fix anything.

The Sabbath is not just an important concept from ancient Jewish culture. It's a practice for us today. One day a week, we stop as an act of remembrance. We remember that God is God and we are human. We have limits. Not everything is up to us.

So one day this week, make a decision to take a Sabbath, and choose the behavior that you are going to stop doing. Even just for one day. Choose a behavior that's not getting you anywhere and yet you remain invested in. What are you serving that is no longer serving you? Choose a Sabbath and notice how the stopping affects you.

• • •

What is one behavior you are taking a Sabbath from this week?

What scares you about letting go of this behavior?

day 26 START FROM A PLACE OF HONESTY INSTEAD OF HIDING

Perhaps it is better to wake up after all, even to suffer, rather than to remain a dupe to illusions all one's life.

—Kate Chopin

I spent a season going to a 12-step group that helped me navigate my emotional life. We, the few of us who attended regularly, circled up our five or so chairs in a smoke-scented classroom and talked about how our inner worlds had become unmanageable. Some people cried. Some people twitched. Some people shook. It was all completely fine, totally normal. Come as you are.

Very quickly into those meetings I learned the upside-down wisdom of taking back our strength by acknowledging our powerlessness. It's absolutely too easy to hide our weakness, compensate for it, even act like it doesn't exist, and try to show the world the slickest version of ourselves. Many of the communities we belong to celebrate those of us who can consistently keep ourselves in life's great Gifted and Talented program, and we can quickly and easily begin to believe that our slickness—our giftedness and talents—is what makes us interesting and worthy.

Through the wisdom of 12-step, I've learned what it means to walk into a room with other people who have come to the end of themselves and were there to talk about it. People drove themselves to a room with fluorescent lighting and lukewarm coffee to confess, to say, "I'm ready to admit I can no longer muscle my way through life or numb my way through life or deny my way through life. I need help. I need to start from a place of honesty instead of hiding."

At these meetings, of all places, I learned more of what it meant to begin again—to watch people decide they no longer deserved to keep hurting themselves and see them regain strength right there in the admission of their weakness.

Do you see how this is so subversive? In our weakness, we become strong. It is only in our refusal to look at our weakness that we remain weak, because all that unexamined tightness has more than enough energy to keep us miserably stuck.

The most beautiful part of it was the honesty, the willingness to sit in the true state of affairs without needing to pretend something else was going on. And this wasn't for the sake of others, for appearances. Truly, when people spoke and told their stories, you got the sense that they had crashed through every last layer of pleasing, posturing, and performing. They were sitting in that room, building a new foundation that had nothing to do with the ego. The ego was no longer in charge.

A death had occurred, the death that always must take place if the journey of transformation is to continue. And now they were ready to live out of something totally new.

Striving was exchanged for surrender.

God, help me to be more honest with you and with myself about . . .

day 27 YOU ARE THE ONE YOU HAVE BEEN WAITING FOR

So Jacob was left alone, and a man wrestled with him till daybreak. When the man saw that he could not overpower him, he touched the socket of Jacob's hip so that his hip was wrenched as he wrestled with the man.

—*Genesis 32:24–25 NIV*

Showing up and staying in the clench requires infinite recommitments to beginning. Coming back to our conversation with God, speaking our anger or our frustration or our longing . . . again . . . even when we think it will yield nothing.

We don't give up. We keep coming to him. Because we are the only ones who can wrestle this out with God. There are no proxies. In the case of our own lives, "we are the ones we have been waiting for," to borrow a beautiful line from poet-activist June Jordan.

When tension begins to build, I can be the kind of person who is scanning the horizon, looking for someone else to come and take care of things for me. A worthy savior.

And I'm not the only one. I was having coffee with a friend the other day and she was telling me about a season in her life when she was completely stuck in a too-tight situation, paralyzed.

"So what was holding you back?" I asked.

"I was waiting for someone to come tell me what my rights were."

No one is coming to save you, a voice says to me in the darkness of dawn. *No one is coming to rescue you.* It was God's voice, though it didn't feel like it at first. At first it felt like how Jacob must have felt—like God was working directly against me. Like the very thing I needed was, now, never going to happen. And these words also felt like they were speaking to a gash that resided in the core of me, a gash that would need to be tended.

The Voice that brought me this news was gentle and calm, not a taunt or a bully. And so I listened. But I wasn't happy about it. I wrestled back, angry and hurt. I wanted the cup to pass and I didn't want to have to face life and adult my way through it. I didn't want any more transformation; I wanted to put my head in the sand.

The Voice kept on. *No one is coming. No one is coming. No one is coming. Except you.* It went on . . . *You have the opportunity to give yourself a gift that no one else can give you. You have the opportunity to take yourself by the hand and walk with yourself through this.*

When you have spent seasons overwhelmed, paralyzed, unsure, and holding back—letting your traumatized nine-year-old self be in charge—it is somewhat revolutionary to have someone whisper in your ear, *You can do this. You really can. Everything you need to step forward, you already have. And I am with you.*

. . .

God, I want to give up. Help me stay in the clench. I wish someone else would come and do this hard work for me. I wish I could abdicate my own life. Keep inviting me into the next, new moment. Keep coaxing me toward wholeness. What I want more than anything is . . .

day 28 A RELIABLE OBSERVER OF MY OWN LIFE

As long as you keep secrets and suppress information, you are fundamentally at war with yourself. . . . The critical issue is allowing yourself to know what you know. That takes an enormous amount of courage.

—Bessel Van Der Kolk, M.D.

I have a strange relationship with "knowing." I want to know, because this seems strong and smart, but I don't always know. In the gap between what I want to know but don't yet, I often believe everyone else has it figured out. One of my most paralyzing Soul Bullies will tell me, "Everyone knows better than you about you."

This is one of the ways I get crippled from the inside out. That Soul Bully is always reiterating, "You are a person who can't possibly know." In other words, I am someone who cannot really be trusted with my own perceptions in a situation.

As a result, I've distrusted myself and my experience of things. Even dismissed my own intuition at times as being misguided. And this is one reason I have wanted someone else to come and tell me what my rights are, tell me how to do my life, tell me which direction to go. I want someone else to validate my perception and my plan of action because, after all, I am not a reliable observer in my own life.

But more than anything, I have wanted to know. And I have wanted to appear that I know. And so I've chased knowing, I think. Likely because I didn't want to face the fear that, deep down, I'm afraid I don't know.

As a result, I have listened to unqualified and unsympathetic advisers, believing they knew better instead of sitting still and listening for myself. I have taken the pulse of others without taking my own or without stopping to listen to God's heartbeat.

What's most important is to remember that each and every one of us is an eligible receiver. I am eligible to receive wisdom, illumination, comfort, and counsel. These are not things I must wait for others to provide for me. These are things I can receive directly from God.

Yes, we need others. We need guides and companions. We need people to raise important points of contention. Without question. And we also need to learn the sound of God's voice and the sound of our own Soul Voice.

• • •

Do you believe that everyone knows better
than you about you and your life?

God, I want to learn to recognize the sound of your voice and I want to learn to recognize the sound of my own Soul Voice. What do you want to say to me today?

day 29 YOU WEREN'T CONSULTED

Forgive yourself for not knowing
what you didn't know before you learned it.
—Elisha Goldstein

Protection helps us avoid dying, but it doesn't necessarily promote real living.

We developed layers of protection and insulation against the world because that's what it took to grow up in a world that was, at times, hostile to us. We adopted strategies, strengths, subtleties in our personalities in order to maneuver through our lives.

This happened. Unavoidably.

We became larger than we needed to be or smaller than we needed to be. We puffed ourselves up or we shrunk ourselves down. We blended in or we stood on the tallest rock and growled with all our teeth showing.

We learned how to change our colors. We figured out how to play dead or squawk aggressively. We got good at waving our feathers, digging a hole, stamping our feet, running for the hills.

These adaptations saved us. We did it. If you're reading this right now, you figured out how to get here.

You figured out how to survive the tumult of your life. You did what you had to do. After all, as I heard someone say recently, "You weren't consulted."

You weren't consulted about your sister's special needs.

You weren't consulted when your parents divorced.

You weren't consulted when the abuse started.

You weren't consulted about your mother's addiction.

You weren't consulted about your father's anger.

You weren't consulted about all the moving.

You weren't consulted when the church split.

You weren't consulted about the mental illness.

You weren't consulted about the financial downturn.

You weren't consulted about the cancer.

You weren't consulted when the mean girls spread lies about you.

You weren't consulted about how you were treated, who listened and who didn't, or what the cost would be.

You weren't consulted.

Nobody took the time, particularly, to ask you if it was all right with you if things blew up.

There you were, needing to survive. And you got incredibly creative. Because that's what we all do. That's what we've all had to do in our own ways. And it's actually a miracle. It's what keeps us on the planet. It's what keeps our species from dying out. It's like a microchip created in us. And it's really, really remarkable.

But (and this is some terrible news I'm about to give you), none of this recuses you.

Because then we become adults who must live in this world with other adults—vulnerably and companionably—and who must also take care of the children in our lives, and the layers that we have packed on so magnificently are now, without much warning, completely in the way of being with these people we love.

These same strategies will cause tension with people we want to be close to. Our props will get in the way of intimacy and connection with others and we will feel lonely. Our ways of being will actually keep us from so much of what we want in life—to be known, to be connected, to belong.

Back then, you weren't consulted. But by the grace of God's free will, now you are. Now you get the chance to speak up and to lean in. It's scared-sacred work: after all this time and all these layers and all those strategies, to let the too-tight skins be removed, to be awakened, to begin again.

• • •

I wasn't consulted when . . .

____

____

____

day 30 TREATING OURSELVES AS WE WOULD A DEAR FRIEND

He finds us and saves us from the thieves of our humanity.

—Brother Mark Brown

If a dear friend—someone I truly love—called me and told me she was feeling stuck and scared and tired, I'd say, "Come over immediately."

When she walked in the door, I would be sure she had all the beverages. Hydration and caffeination. I would know how she likes her coffee and I'd have it waiting for her. I'd know if she likes ice water, water with no ice, or sparkling water. And I'd have it waiting for her. I'd take out (and actually light) the expensive Anthropologie candle (the one that costs $6 a minute to burn) and I'd pet her arm.

I wouldn't say, "Gah, do you know how many times you've needed prayer this month? You are such a mess. I can't *take* it anymore." No, I'd meet her in the middle. I'd sit with her. I'd love her. I'd listen. I'd suspend judgment or clever advice. I'd be a witness to her struggle so she would know she isn't alone.

But how often do I sit with myself in this way? How often do I maintain this posture with myself? Don't I always assume that bullying, prodding, and degrading are the ways into change when it comes to me? If I can just be hard enough on myself, I will get it this time.

Sometimes I sit down and make two lists:

1. How do I think about, talk about, and talk to my dear friends?
2. How do I think about, talk about, and talk to myself?

It's actually a very telling exercise.

For far too many of us, though certainly not all of us, our first instinct is to starve, push, condemn, convict, beat up, criticize, scold, demean, lecture ourselves into new territory. *If I can just convince myself of how bad I am, then I will make changes.*

This is slavery. And it will not last.

We do not punish ourselves into transformation. We do not begin again by refusing to forgive ourselves. I've come to believe that we make lasting changes because we know, somewhere inside us, that we are invited into more.

We do not begin again by refusing to forgive ourselves.

One of the meanings of the word *forgive* is "to give up the desire or power to punish."[1] Man. Giving up the desire or power to punish ourselves is taking ourselves down from the giant hook of regret.

Forgiving ourselves for covering up, holding up, propping up . . . when what was needed was opening up. We didn't know. Or if we did, we just weren't ready. Can we forgive ourselves for being where we *are* and not where we wish were? Can we see that we are inching toward where we always hoped we could be?

There are so few things in life we can control, but one thing we can control is how we treat ourselves and that one thing can change everything.

• • •

1. How do I think about, talk about, and talk to my dear friends?

____

____

____

2. How do I think about, talk about, and talk to myself?

____

____

____

day 31 THE MYSTERY OF TRANSFORMATION

God said to Gideon, "Take your father's best seven-year-old bull, the prime one. Tear down your father's Baal altar and chop down the Asherah fertility pole beside it. Then build an altar to God, your God, on the top of this hill. Take the prime bull and present it as a Whole-Burnt-Offering, using firewood from the Asherah pole that you cut down."

—Judges 6:25–26

Change, Father Richard Rohr says, is typically when something new begins. But the mystery of transformation is something different. Transformation is "not when something new begins but when something old falls apart."[1] And this disorientation of things falling apart is what nudges us into new ways of thinking. Otherwise, perhaps we would never go on our own volition.

Everything in us resists the old falling apart.

> The pain of something old falling apart—chaos—invites the soul to listen at a deeper level. It invites and sometimes forces the soul to go to a new place because the old place is falling apart. Otherwise most of us would never go to a new place. . . . You will do anything to keep the old thing from falling apart.[2]

The problem with allowing the old to fall apart is that we are afraid of what it's going to cost us. And like many of you, I don't know if I have it in me to pay.

The cost, to me, would be a more complete surrender than I had previously experienced, which means a deeper trust than I have ever allowed myself to practice. And what I can tell you now, at the risk of getting ahead of myself, is that the anticipation of all this was much more difficult than the actual passage through. The passage through ended up being a relief. The anticipation of pain, the fear of being in pain, was the hardest part.

We see that our way of doing or being is no longer working, and so we are confronted with either nurturing it, gripping it, holding tightly to it, attaching ourselves even more deeply to it—or unhanding it.

Maybe the things you are serving feel as though they *are* still serving you. This is fine. You are where you are, and you cannot be where you are not. And you are not yet ready.

Someday, though, you may be walking down the street, innocuously, and you will all of a sudden have an epiphany. You will realize that these things actually aren't serving you in any way:

Your keeping the peace at all costs, even in a toxic situation

Your crowd-building

Your need to keep everyone happy

Your clinging to certainty

Your harbored resentment

Your need to appear competent

Your belief in the voices of self-loathing and self-bullying

You'll be doing the most mundane thing, and *shazam!*, the faraway thing you have been waiting for will arrive—maybe because you created a soft place for it to land—and you will know something you did not know the minute previously. You will know that you are deeply entrenched in a relationship with some behavior or substance or person or past, and you have been giving it your all, and it is giving you nothing but trouble in return.

And you will be ready.

• • •

Do you sense an invitation to let something old fall apart?
What is your resistance?

____

____

____

____

____

____

day 32 STARVE THE STRAY CATS

Search me, O God, and know my heart;
Try me and know my anxious thoughts;
And see if there be any hurtful way in me,
And lead me in the everlasting way.
—Psalm 139:23–24 NASB

God asked me some questions I was not ready for. He said, *What if shame isn't your greatest enemy after all? What if shame is actually your dearest friend? What if you are more attached to this shame-stance than you realize? What if your greatest fear is being rid of it? What would you have then, if you didn't have this self-condemnation?*

Shame's vicious voice is comforting to me in a weird way. It is the voice I recognize more than any other. What would I be left with if it was no longer with me?

You are allowed to leave it, Leeana. Unhook from it. Not need it anymore. You are allowed to believe something else. You are allowed to be comfortable with your own strength.

Starving shame is hard. All I want to do is feed it. Buy into its story. Over and over again. I believe, like with the stray cat, if I feed it, it will go away. But what happens? It now knows where its nourishment is coming from and so it stays on. Happily. Crying for more food. Warm milk. Pawing at the door. Back for more. Let me in. Let me in. Let me in. Let me curl up on your couch and warm your feet forever.

This is not the work we are doing. We are not feeding the stray cats. Because it is never enough. They are never appeased. They are never filled.

Once you begin to confront your own attachments, securities, pet pathologies, and once you sense God inviting you to hand them to him, you will know something transformative is happening. *But transformation always requires us to leave something behind.* And that's never easy.

This has nothing to do with behaving better, cleaning up our act. This is simply about granting God access to each layer of ourselves, one by one, as we are able. This is opening up instead of covering up. Honesty before God.

God has come to me in the dark of morning and suggested my attachment. He's named something for me—that I am closer to shame than I wanted to admit—and as I drink down my coffee and stare out the window beyond the hills as the rose-gold is starting to streak the sky, I know what I didn't know the minute previously.

My journey isn't about either eradicating shame or being subject to it. My journey, for the foreseeable future, is going to be the daily, hourly, minute-to-minute surrender of shame. Admitting, over and over again, my tendency to want to nourish those stray cats and, instead, allowing God to speak over me.

• • •

Fill in the blank:

What if ______________________________ isn't your greatest enemy after all?

What if ______________________________ is actually your dearest friend?

God, is there anything you want to say to me about this stray cat I'm nourishing?

____

____

____

____

____

____

____

day 33 SPEAK LOUDER

Let go
Let fly
Forget
You've listened long enough
Now, strike your note
—*Seamus Heaney*

On my fortieth birthday, my friend Wanida slid a little black box across the table to me. Wanida has the spiritual gift of "Giving MAC Makeup." Not sure if you've heard of this one. I think there's an obscure reference to it somewhere in the New Testament. Anyway, Wanida slid this slick black lipstick box to me across the table. I opened it and twisted the tube to reveal a gorgeous shade of hot pink. I winked at her, as she knows I love this color. But that wasn't it. She winked back and motioned to me to turn it over and see the name of the lipstick color.

I flipped the tube on its end and these words were looking back at me:

SPEAK LOUDER

In all caps. My eyes filled and Wanida said, "Speak louder. We need to hear your voice."

I knew what she meant, and it wasn't about volume. She meant, Don't be that guy who buried everything he was given because he was afraid of being a disappointment. She was saying, "Let it ride, and let's see what happens."

Speaking louder is not about being belligerent or brash. It's about knowing the sound of our own voice and knowing when we need to be quiet and when we need to be courageous.

We need to spend a robust amount of time listening. More than we think. But don't listen as a means of hiding. Don't let listening paralyze you.

Is it time for you to strike *your* note?

• • •

The wise listen when it's time to listen and speak when it's time to speak. Is there a situation in your life where you might need to speak louder?

____

____

____

____

____

day 34 THRESHOLD

The horizon leans forward
offering you space to place new steps
of change.

—Maya Angelou

The word *threshold* has convoluted origins. It quite literally means "point of entering," but the etymology suggests that a threshold may have been "a threshing area adjacent to a living area of a house."[1] A place where the work was done, where the wheat was separated from the chaff.

Chaff is the inedible, scaly skin that surrounds the edible goodness of the crop. Threshing removes this skin. So the threshing area was the place where the work of separation was done. The work of shedding. Like Eustace, undragoned, as Aslan removed one self-protecting dragon skin after the other until Eustace was transformed back into a boy.[2] Crossing the threshold is often about shedding, not adding.

When you do this work, when you decide to do this sacred work, you will come to a point at which you are at an impasse. You will be ready to grow, super-duper gung ho about becoming the more brazen you. And then you will begin to realize that you have ways of being and ways of relating that will not allow for this becoming. You will be so ready until you see what must be lost in order for you to be found.

And it's a bit of a shocker, can I just say.

It will start deep down, a low knowing. You will know what needs to change. Your wise old woman within will join hands with God and they will begin to collude. They will lean on your soul, applying a gentle pressure. They will create just enough tension to get your attention. And so, right there, you will be given an invitation, a choice.

They will tell you it is time, but only if you want it to be. They will not coerce you into anything. They'll just show you that a door has presented itself and you are now aware of it. You must choose to walk through, walk across the threshold of shedding and separating, or freeze, or walk away.

God doesn't grow weary of your winding path.

Whatever you choose, they will be with you.

You will not be left or abandoned. God will not be disgusted with you. Ever. In that way, God is not like the people in your life. God doesn't tire of your struggle and your back-and-forth and your uncertainty. God doesn't grow weary of your winding path.

The walking-through or walking-away decision will likely come again. I think God is continually inviting us into this work—because he is good and because he loves us—but he lets us decide if we are ready. And it's OK if we're not. It's OK if we're not ready.

When we are ready, we will still be scared and reluctant and queasy, but we will *know*. We will know deep down that it is time, that we are willing, and that in order for the new thing to be born, an old thing will need to die.

• • •

God, give me the courage to cross the threshold you have brought me to. Help me to remember . . .

day 35 BRING HER TO ME

In returning and rest you shall be saved.
—Isaiah 30:15 NKJV

Inside me, there is a nine-year-old me who is looking at life like a deer in the headlights. She's made entirely of a thousand raw nerve endings. She's both frozen and skittish, and she's deeply needy. She wants my time and my attention and my constant care. And she *deserves* all the love in the entire world. She *deserves* time and attention and constant care. Do you, too, know this version of yourself? The one stuck in a time where nothing was in her control?

There's just one problem: *I cannot give her everything she needs.* And neither can you.

I cannot off-load this precious me I am carrying around. Not even for a second. She needs my constant vigilance and watchful eye. She cannot withstand abandonment. But her need is swallowing me whole.

God whispers to me as gently as possible in that early morning:

You are allowed to care for her and move beyond her. You are not leaving her. You are not abandoning her. You are honoring her.

You are rescuing her. You believe that if you grow beyond her, she will be forgotten, that her story will be forgotten. She needs love and attention, yes, but she is not where you end.

I will take care of her. You do not have to carry her. Bring her to me. I will take care of her so you can walk into the world freely and with open arms.

Come to me and I will give you rest.

Bring her to me. She is precious and wounded and wide-eyed and wild-eyed and I will care for her so that you can keep going. Go, Leeana. Go. Be free.

She is so fragile, practically injured. Keeping up with her and taking care of her is exhausting me.

Yes, bring her to me and I will meet her needs. Nothing you can do will heal her except bringing her to me. Her healing will also heal you.

You are afraid to betray her. You are the only one who can bring her to me. No one else has that right or ability. I cannot even come and take her from you. You must bring her to me. Surrender her. You must choose if you're ready. There is a part of you that feels most safe when you are with her, nursing her wounds. You have purpose and distraction. But it's keeping you from other things now. You have tended to her. You have loved her. You have watched her, vigilantly. Now it's my turn. Bring her to me so I can send you out.

You can give yourself a gift that no one else can give you. In return, I will give you a gift too. Freedom.

Are you ready?

God invited me to take her off my back and put her down in front of me, where I had to look at her. Really look at her. Which I did not want to do. FOR THE LIFE OF ME. This meant detaching from her enough to actually look at her because that is what she needed most, why she was globbed on to my back in the first place. She needed to be seen, listened to, honored, not just hoisted up and carried. But if you're like me, you will do anything to avoid having to look at this deeply frozen part of yourself. It's so scary.

Then God invites me, in the dark of one random Monday morning, to pick up my fragile nine-year-old self and bring her to him. Put her in his arms. Let him care for her. I am terrified, of course, because I do not want to leave her. I do not want to abandon her. And he says, *Bring her to me.*

I do, because I want to learn how to love someone or something without losing myself in their power.

• • •

Is there a young, fragile, vulnerable part of you that is begging for all of your resources and attention? How old is that part of you? What happened to her?

day 36 THE THIRD WAY

There is no fear in love. But perfect love drives out fear, because fear has to do with punishment. The one who fears is not made perfect in love.

—1 John 4:18 NIV

In this scared-sacred work of becoming, the Soul Bullies plant endless false dichotomies, skewing our thinking, so that we stay stuck: "You can either have approval or you can have intimacy. You can either confront issues and be consumed or you can avoid issues and be paralyzed. You can either use your voice and make people mad or silence your voice and keep people happy."

Either/or thinking is a red flag, an indication that our thoughts and feelings are under the control of fear and not Love. When I back myself into either/or thinking, it is always a lose-lose: total demise or total denial.

Those are my only two choices, neither of which is particularly appealing. When we do this, we start to get very anxious, because our minds and bodies know we have created a too-tight system. No matter which path we take, we can't win, which is a suffocating reality.

But Love offers us a different way of thinking altogether, one that is transcendent and not transactional.

Love offers us a third way. *Via media* is Latin for the middle way, the narrow path that cuts between our dichotomies and dualistic thinking.

- The path to healing and becoming always takes the *via media*, the very narrow way that insists life, real living, is somehow inextricably linked to surrender.

The narrow way requires letting go, burning down, and maybe most of all, trusting in something beyond what we can see.

• • •

God, I am caught in either/or thinking. Please show me the third way.

____

____

____

____

____

day 37 THE COMFORT WE CRAVE

You are the place where I stand on the day when my feet are sore.

—Wes Carry

Elle, my seven-year-old, asks me, "Mom, are you tired?"

"Yes, Elle, I am tired," I say. "How did you know?"

"Because you're wearing all soft clothes."

I look down and realize she's absolutely right. I am wearing, up to and including my shoes, "all soft clothes."

I'm writing this from the Messy Middle, a place that exists somewhere between "Beginning" and "End." The Messy Middle is undefined, murky, and requires the practice of surrender, which is tiring business. So, yes, if you see me around town, you might notice that just the other week I was wearing plaid socks with Birkenstocks. I'd never done that before, but it just seemed right. Or you might see me in, essentially, pajamas, with a fur vest. Because, apparently, when I get tired, I reach for all soft clothes.

Comfort.

I think the word is comfort. When life changes, when circumstances aren't as we expected, when we are navigating new territory, we need comfort. We can look a lot of different places for comfort—some helpful, some not. (For example, distractions rarely deliver the comfort we crave.)

So then, where might comfort—true comfort, which is solace, help, consolation, strength—be found?

God holds us and meets us and comforts us in so many different ways. Earlier this week I had a big speaking engagement. I was feeling depleted and asking God for his strength to move in on my weakness because that's how I felt: weak. I was sitting at my table and these four Warrior Sisters just showed up, unannounced. I've known these girls forever. Decades. These four are a part of my everyday tribe. And they walked in and sat down at my table like they just happened to be in the neighborhood (even though they all drove 45 minutes out of their way to be there).

So the beautiful truth is that God holds us, he comforts us, he comes to us. Sometimes it's in the form of four fabulous friends. Sometimes it's in the form of his Word—alive and awakening—spoken right into our souls. Sometimes his comfort comes in the form of Ugg boots and a stretch waistband. Because when we are weak, he really shines.

• • •

How has God brought you unexpected comfort recently?

____

____

____

day 38 LOVE ANYWAY

No matter what I say, what I believe, and what I do, I'm bankrupt without love.

—1 Corinthians 13:3

I do not know why impossible things happen. Impossible things have happened in my life over the last year. Things I didn't choose. Impossible things have likely happened in your life or in the life of someone you love, and it feels like a sucker punch, really.

I just got the news that a close friend is very ill and is not expected to live. I cannot understand how someone with so much to live for, someone with so much vibrancy and vitality, could be taken from us. Just like that. Without anyone really having much of a say.

I do not know how, despite incredible pain and loss, we go on. But we do. Not in the same way as before. Perhaps with a limp. But we continue.

For most of us who keep walking into the next, new moment, it is because we have decided to love anyway.

We have decided that no matter the loss and the pain and the disappointment, love is still worth giving and receiving. Love is still the most powerful force there is.

When we are grieving and angry and trying to make sense of the senseless, we can be tempted to think it's not worth it. It's not worth putting our hearts and our lives out into the world. It's not worth believing in someone else or allowing them to believe in us.

I bought myself a sweatshirt that says "LOVE ANYWAY" on it and I've been wearing it around a lot . . . a reminder that love does more than anger and resentment ever could. Love is a workhorse and whisper and wind, and it is always worth our time.

• • •

Have you been hurt? Are you tempted to turn off love in your life? What does God want to say to you about loving anyway?

____

____

____

____

____

____

day 39 NEW NORMAL

If you are present to the now, and you are present in love, you are present to God.

—*Thomas Merton*

I'm looking at all of you who are navigating any kind of New Normal right now. A New Normal is a situation that is requiring us to flex or pivot or let go (noooooo!) of expectations. I'm so sorry, and I completely get it. Some years we have limits we didn't have before. Some years we have new circumstances and new realities to adjust to.

Being "present" is all the rage, a buzzword even, but we don't always acknowledge the spiritual, emotional, mental, and physical discipline required to stay present, especially when the present is uncertain, unresolved, or just plain new.

New Normals are clumsy and tiring because they are uncharted. Some years we are moving. Some years we are sick. Some years we are without those who made everything feel normal. Some years we have a new baby or a new puppy. Some years we have kids away for any number of reasons. Some years we have less money than we've ever had. Some years we have brand-new faces around our table.

If any of this is you this year, I see you. And me too. Here we are. And here's what I know for sure. We are held. It's all held. All the insanity and sadness and adjusting and hope and grief . . . everything is held. God-hands are surrounding us.

And within those God-hands is enough space for an endless range of experiences and emotions, so go ahead and name what it all looks like and feels like for you this year. All the loss, all the gains, all the remember-whens, and the maybe-soons.

Remembrance of what has been. Hope for what will be. Vigil for the miles that stretch between.

• • •

God, give me the grace to be where my feet are, to be right in the middle of this New Normal. And give me the words to name what this New Normal is and how it is affecting me and the people I love.

My New Normal is . . .

____

____

____

____

____

day 40 WHO IS HOLDING HOPE FOR YOU?

We who have run for our very lives to God have every reason to grab the promised hope with both hands and never let go.

—Hebrews 6:18

Who is holding hope for you? Recently someone sent me a text that was filled with hope. The kind of hope that's hard for me to hold right now, if I'm being totally honest. And yet, reading her words has been such an incredible comfort to me, like I can draft off her momentum.

Father Richard Rohr says, "Hope is the patient and trustful willingness to live without closure, without resolution, and still be content and even happy because our Satisfaction is now at another level, and our Source is beyond ourselves."[1]

So then hope is our patient and trustful willingness to live in the Messy Middles with assurance that our lives are held by Someone far greater than us. Sounds really hard to me, right about now. How about you?

Sometimes we just don't have the capacity or the stamina or even the desire to hold on to hope, and yet I believe hopelessness is certainly not a better alternative.

Is there someone in your life who could hold hope for you on the days when you don't have the capacity? It's a gift to return to their words and know that someone is believing on your behalf.

• • •

It's hard for me to have hope about . . .

____

____

____

Is there someone who could hold hope for you?

____

____

____

day 41 YOU ARE NOT YOUR CIRCUMSTANCES

Because of the LORD's great love we are not consumed, for his compassions never fail. They are new every morning; great is your faithfulness.
—Lamentations 3:22–23 NIV

I spoke to an amazing group of women recently, and we talked about the word *brazen* and how it means "unashamed" and "unapologetic." We talked about receiving our identity, reclaiming our voices, and recovering our souls, which is all a part of the brazen work of coming out of hiding and honoring who we are created to be.

Hide or *honor*. We get to choose, but I believe God is always inviting us to honor the gold in each of us. Genesis 3 tells the story of the fall, and it's easy to forget that the story starts two chapters earlier when God formed us from dust. The shaming Soul Bullies want to keep us small and hidden and they want us to live the Genesis 3 story every single day. But I don't believe the most essential thing about us is that we are flawed.

I believe the most essential thing about us is that we were made in the image of God. On the day of creation, God put his hands in the wet concrete of our souls and said, It is good. Actually, it is *very* good.

It's easy for us to forget this image of God that sits at our core because of all the crazy stuff that happens in our lives. Things we do. Things others do to us. And we begin to believe that we are what is happening to us at any given moment.

God reminded me just the other day, *Leeana, YOU are not your circumstances.*

And I want to pass that along to you as well. Your circumstances do not define you. God does. So no matter how messy the Messy Middle is that you're in right now, I believe there is a part of you that is deeper and more essential than anything you are going through.

On the day of creation, God put his hands in he wet concrete of our souls and said, It is good. Actually, it is very good.

Your issues are not your identity. THANK GOD. Something runs deeper in us than any circumstance. So *where* you are right now, *where* I am right now, is not *who* we are. Isn't that everything?

It is with unending hope that I repeat what is said in Lamentations 3:22–23. Because of God's great love, we are not consumed. Circumstances cannot consume us. The Soul Bullies cannot consume us. Shame cannot consume us. Fear cannot consume us.

Something deep and original and enduring in us exists apart from all of the ick and insanity of life. And when we forget, when we forget that our story started in Genesis 1 with God calling us forth and calling us good, we can remind ourselves by calling upon his new-every-morning mercies to help us remember who we really are. Created. Beloved. Brazen.

Remember who you are.

You are not abuse. You are not anxiety. You are not depression. You are not infertility. You are not divorce. You are not abortion. You are not addiction. You are not failure. You are not your body. You are not the beige. You are the beloved, precious soul. The brazen, beautiful beloved.

...

I am not . . .

____

____

____

I am . . .

____

____

____

day 42 HOMES FOR THE HOMELESS

God makes homes for the homeless.

—Psalm 68:6

There are a lot of different ways to be homeless, to feel displaced in your own life. Relationally homeless. Spiritually homeless. Physically homeless. Professionally homeless. Even emotionally homeless, as waves of tragedy and violence fill this world we are trying to live in and love in.

Homelessness is disorienting. Where do I belong? Who are my people? What belongs to me? What is my place? Where can I rest? We're stuck lurking in no-man's-land.

What do we do when we don't feel tethered, grounded, placed?

The above Scripture from Psalm 68 has long been a favorite of mine: "God makes homes for the homeless." What a beautiful piece of poetry. Have you experienced this? Radical displacement followed by God finding you, reaching out to you, and building you a shelter? Maybe the shelter wasn't the mansion on the hill you were hoping for. Maybe it was a lean-to, cobbled together out of the most unlikely sources. But extraordinarily beautiful in its own way because it was something made from nothing. Resurrection.

I remember when our family moved overseas with two toddlers and a new baby on the way, and the reality of displacement burned in my chest every day. To the point that I felt desperate at times. While we were there, God found me in the strangest possible ways. Hot pink bougainvillea. Handmade rugs. A tiny Ethiopian nanny. A friend. A new baby born in a room where a huge arrow pointed to Mecca and a prayer rug hid in the bedside table.

He has the wildest ways of finding us. Of sheltering us. Of building us a home when we are refugees in our own lives.

After dropping my kids off at school this morning, I parked in the driveway and passed one of the two potted bougainvillea flanking the garage door. The one on the right is blooming, healthy, abundant. The one on the left is scraggly, bony, maybe even dying. But at the end of a long, brown, lifeless limb was a cluster of irreverent fuchsia blooms.

How is this possible? I don't totally know or understand, except to say that I think this is somehow one of the most important things we can learn in life: He makes beautiful things out of barrenness. He makes homes for the homeless. And he often does it against all odds.

If you are feeling homeless today in any way—not sure where you're going to live professionally or relationally or emotionally or physically—you're not alone, and God has not forgotten. He can spin beauty out of dust. That's his way. And personally, I'm holding him to it.

• • •

God, I feel homeless because . . .

How is God cobbling together an unlikely shelter for you in this season of your life?

day 43 APPROVAL ISN'T LOVE

Through the Spirit, Christ offered himself as an unblemished sacrifice, freeing us from all those dead-end efforts to make ourselves respectable, so that we can live all out for God.

—Hebrews 9:15

I had secretly thought, in a place that I could not unlock, the best I could hope for in life was approval. I'd be lucky to get approval, and if I were to garner it, this sanction, this permission, this endorsement from the world would be enough.

Maybe it wasn't as good as the stuff other people got. Love, for example. But hey, if you can't have love, approval ain't bad. Right?

Eugene Peterson writes about the ecstasy of crowds, how crowds can be a way we attempt to transcend our humanity. Like drug and alcohol abuse and illicit sex, crowds are a way we try to make ourselves feel better about ourselves. Not just the ecstasy of an in-person crowd, but also the ecstasy of an online crowd. Crowds feel good. Crowds clap and yell their approval.

But approval isn't love.

Contact isn't connection.

Image isn't intimacy.

None of this approval-seeking is the real problem, though. *The down-deep problem is that somewhere along the way we began believing the idea that we were never going to get love.*

I am just now quiet enough, still enough, to hear this.

Are you seeking approval when deep down, what you have wanted and needed all along is love?

Is it possible that all the seeking and striving is the very thing standing in the way of the love you are longing for?

The beautiful poet David Whyte talks about each of us having our own doorway of vulnerability and that part of our life's work is to walk through it. The root of the word *vulnerable* is the Latin *vulneras*, which means "wound." And so when we are vulnerable we are showing our wounds to the world (not just our slick exteriors), and this is how we connect, heal, and ultimately experience love.

The temptation is to be impressive. The invitation is to be honest.

• • •

God, show me the ways I am seeking approval over love.

___

___

___

day 44 OFFERING EVERYDAY LIFE

So here's what I want you to do, God helping you: Take your everyday, ordinary life—your sleeping, eating, going-to-work, and walking-around life—and place it before God as an offering. Embracing what God does for you is the best thing you can do for him.

—Romans 12:1–2

I begin brushing Lane's wet hair, as gently as I can because she shrieks like a cat if I don't, and then I turn the blow dryer on high. I run the brush through her hair, following it with the dryer, shaking out the excess water in the next section.

Her brown hair gains a copper sheen as it dries.

I look, alternately, from my work with the brush to her reflection in the mirror. She is inspecting my work, turning her head from side to side to see how smooth her hair has become. She's pleased. I can tell. We smile at each other in the mirror.

I am there. I am there for all of it.

As our inner life feels tight and restrictive, we go looking for ways to broaden it externally. As our inner life expands and we begin to come home to ourselves, we do not need the pace and proving and productivity of the external life like we once did.

It keeps calling me: a slightly smaller external life, and a slightly larger interior life.

Tending—directing one's mind and energies toward, literally stretching toward, to pay attention—is the ritual of beginning again, and it is impossible to tend when we are frantic. So when I feel this longing to tend to Lane's scrambled hair and I notice the color changing as I dry it, I know something has almost imperceptibly begun shifting.

I am not running circles around my life, trying to make it all better. I'm standing in the middle of it. And I know I am where I belong.

• • •

God, help me invest in my interior life with the same energy that I invest in my external life.

Close your eyes and take three deep breaths. Ask God to show you one thing you could tend today—something small and mundane—and one thing you could let go of—something that seems urgent but may not necessarily be.

____

____

____

day 45 TWILIGHT COMES TWICE

Show me a day when the world wasn't new.

—Sister Barbara Hance

When I was minutes out of graduate school and brand-newly twenty-four years old, I drove from West Virginia, where I had been in school, down to Virginia to pick up my little brother from college, home to San Diego, and then I slept for an entire day. When I woke up, I found a book my mom left on my nightstand. A gift. *Twilight Comes Twice*. It's a children's book about dawn and dusk, a simple reminder that the sun goes down and the sun comes up. Every day. And twice, in between, we get the gift of these golden hours, these pockets of waking up and winding down.

No matter how beautiful and epic and glorious life is right now, the sun goes down. And no matter how ugly and rejecting and hurtful life is right now, the sun comes up. Something about this saved me then and saves me now. I was young and starting over geographically and professionally and relationally. But more than that, the very rhythm of creation was reminding me that it wasn't all up to me. Something was going on that was beyond me, behind me, below me, beside me.

And I just needed to join it, fall into it, beginning again and again and again.

I could join or I could resist. But either way, the sun would set and the sun would rise—with or without me. I could try to outrun the sun with my superhuman striving. I could try to hide in the dark with my subhuman shame. But the invitation, then and now, was to join the rhythm of creation, which is to be what we were simply and profoundly created to be . . . human.

If you're in the dark, you can begin again. And if you're in the broad side of the light, you will still need to begin again.

Human. In all its extraordinary everyday ordinariness.

If I am failing, stuck, and paralyzed, I always have the opportunity to begin again. And if I am winning, elated, and propelled, I still must begin again. None of us is too far gone, in the same way that none of us has arrived. This is reorienting to the core.

Could you and I join the rhythm of twice-a-day twilight that reminds us there are gifts in both the light and dark—illumination and stillness? If you're in the dark, you can begin again. And if you're in the broad side of the light, you will still need to begin again. This is how we practice being human.

Twilight comes twice.

Whether we are in crisis or chaos or calm, hope or disappointment, burial or resurrection, ordinariness or extraordinariness, we can—because of the inexhaustible grace of God—begin again.

. . .

Am I practicing the rhythm of light and dark, productivity and stillness?

day 46 WHAT IT MEANS TO BE HUMAN

For grace to be grace, it must give us things we didn't know we needed and take us places where we didn't know we didn't want to go.

—Kathleen Norris

We probably already had an inkling of where our journey was headed. We knew we were on an unsustainable ride. We just weren't ready to see. We just hadn't fully embraced the knowing. We needed the time in the darkness. And it's all OK, I'm learning. It's our process. It's our process of not just accepting our circumstances but accepting our humanity and all the glorious limitations that accompany being human.

Here's what it means to be human: I cannot see everything, I cannot know everything, I cannot be awake to everything. And it's OK. It doesn't mean I'm lost or worthless. It means I will forever be in need of God, of a guide (or two), of a gang of Warrior Sisters, of coffee at the kitchen table at 5:00 a.m., of surrendering to the invitation—even if it doesn't all make perfect sense.

We're still trying to decide, each day, if God can be trusted. We're still beginning again most days, because we get our hands back on our own lives, and then we see that we have no real big winning ideas without being connected to the Source.

The way we forgive ourselves, hang in there with ourselves, grieve and celebrate in the same breath is to . . . begin again. This is the simplest and most profound truth I come back to.

We love the idea of doing things once and for all, but this is not where meaning is found. We don't take Communion once and for all. We don't love our spouse once and for all. We don't parent once and for all. We don't do the dishes or the laundry or the vacuuming once and for all. We don't read, endure the commute, or shave our legs once and for all.

We return—in what becomes a sacred connection—to the mundane task, to the moment. And then we do it again. Over and over. Again. This is the raw material of our living. And none of it is to be overlooked.

This is not insanity or hilarity or nuisance or idiocy. This is the task of humanity. To return. To reinvest. To breathe. To begin again. The focus is on the process, the participation, not the product. Ever.

• • •

What does it look like when you are staying engaged and invested in your life?

---

day 47 IT'S A DISTRACTION—NOTHING MORE, NOTHING LESS

Whether you turn to the right or to the left, your ears will hear a voice behind you, saying, "This is the way; walk in it."

—Isaiah 30:21 NIV

The other morning I got the kids settled at school and ran back home to get changed for a speaking engagement, only to find a sprinkler had erupted and a geyser was gushing behind our garage.

Wouldn't you know it, on that one day a week when I shower.

It was the worst possible timing for something like this to happen, which is just so like life . . . the unfortunate event disrupts us and delays us and derails us when we are in our favorite shoes and we finally got our hair done.

I arrived at the event feeling a little teetery and tottery, and the Soul Bullies were having their usual heyday. When my day takes a turn for the worse is often when the bullies are at their harrowing best.

This is what you might call a perfect storm, the kind of disruption that turns into far more than a shooting stream of water in the yard. Somehow, this sprinkler leak became the evidence that I was on an entirely wrong and completely misguided path in my life. What was at first a maintenance issue is now a metaphor. My life is out of control, one giant mudslide of a mess.

And without totally realizing what we've done, we give in to the geysers. We say, "You're right. What was I thinking? Walking out into the world is a bad idea. Showing up is insane. Creating is nuts. Using my voice is a liability. I'm going to just go back in the house and rehearse how the universe is conspiring against me."

Do you know what the geysers are? They are distractions. They are the way the dark forces of this world try to keep the gorgeous thing from being born. Not annihilation, just simply distraction. If these distracting forces can shift our focus from soul-tending to mini-crisis, they know we're off the scent.

What geyser in your life is going off—histrionically waving its obnoxious hands—trying to get you to tend to it instead of what you really need to be working on?

"Over here!" it yells. "Over here! Look at me!"

But you can walk right past that distraction and chuckle because you've got that geyser's number.

You are not going to allow the mess to make you feel overly responsible for a sprinkler head and underresponsible for your own soul. When it begins whining for your attention, you do what my friend Linsey says to do. You say, "Sorry. This time, I'm choosing me."

• • •

Distractions can come in all shapes, sizes, colors, and disguises. Is there something in your life that is unworthy of your time and attention and yet it is consuming all of both?

God, show me what is worthy of my time and attention and what is simply a distraction.

day 48 WHO HAS THE ENERGY?

Don't run from suffering; embrace it. Follow me and I'll show you how. Self-help is no help at all. Self-sacrifice is the way, my way, to finding yourself, your true self.

—Luke 9:24

The energy to begin again cannot come from us. We cannot be the source. Beginning again cannot be one more thing we are striving to do. Because we, in and of ourselves, do not have the necessary energy. For example:

Who has the energy to fight for a marriage day after day, month after month, year after year . . . when things have been hard for so long and the patterns and cycles don't seem to be resolving into health and happiness and ease . . . when everyone's tired and stretched and bouncing off each other?

Who has the energy to begin again with children? To reengage in the same schedule and the same squabbles and the same snacks every day, day after day? Like a run-on sentence. When we know the time is slipping through our fingers and we will want these days back? Who in the world has the determination to give them everything we want to give them when we feel like we don't have anything? How can family life feel like it's evaporating one second and then pond water the next?

Who has the energy to begin again professionally, when the project didn't pan out or the exposure was public or we feel like we're running out of time? Who can get back up and use these feelings of failure and rejection as fuel for something new?

Who has the energy to begin again with life's responsibilities? We write the check this month, knowing we will have to do it all over again the next. We fold the last load of laundry even as the next is piling up. We put all the dishes away even as the next meal is ready to be made. What gives us the capacity to begin again when repetition seems like the most impossible task, like banging your head against a wall instead of movement?

Who has the energy to begin again with her body, which seems to betray her and yell at her and need, need, need? Who can stand the inner work required to build a body from the inside out?

And who has the energy to begin again with herself? To back out of the self-versus-self antagonism and do the very difficult work of treating herself like a companion instead of a critic? Who has the capacity to sit compassionately with herself, over and over again, when all she wants to do is condemn? Who among us has the Love within to forgive herself again and again?

Who can open their hurting heart that has clamped shut yet again? Who could let God in once again, even though our faith has not protected us from disappointment, maybe even devastation, maybe even disaster? When we've been burned by people who said they believed too? Who could have the resilience and resolve to go on believing when faith hasn't seemed to produce much of anything? Or so it feels today.

I'll tell you who: none of us.

Some of us are trying. We're trying so hard. We are on our best behavior, implementing our most efficient strategies. We are mastering the art of stamina and we are strong, strong, strong. We are as capable as they get and we can handle hard things.

But our strength will not be what fuels our capacity to step into each next, new moment. God's love and our surrender to his love are the only way.

• • •

God, my "try" is running out of steam. Please give me a new dose of trust today, the kind that can only come from you. I am opening my hands to your plan and your timing and your love.

day 49 THE SPIRITUAL DISCIPLINE OF DISAPPOINTING PEOPLE

Since this is the kind of life we have chosen, the life of the Spirit, let us make sure that we do not just hold it as an idea in our heads or a sentiment in our hearts, but work out its implications in every detail of our lives.

—Galatians 5:25

I heard someone say recently that when we begin to gain liberation, when we begin to unhook our worth and our meaning from what we produce and how "good" we are, those who are still locked in this system, those who are not-yet-free, will be deeply bothered by our audacity. Even unknowingly, they will come after us, because we have broken the understood rules of the tribe.

We are no longer trading our effort and energy for love. Somehow, by the grace of God, we got it. We found out the good news that we are OK and we are loved no matter what. *Nothing can separate us from the love of God (Rom. 8:38–39).* But those who haven't yet ingested that good news are tied up and chained, and when they see us leaving the merit system that we are all supposed to be living by, earning, earning, earning, well, they don't like it that someone else may have found another way. We are breaking the understood rules.

This is where the spiritual discipline of disappointing people really shines. We begin to see that we cannot follow God's invitation of liberation for us and also please everyone. It's just not possible. Some days we will get up and we will live fully out of the knowledge that we are loved and "in" no matter what, and we will let the chips fall where they may. Other days, we will scamper around like a spooked colt, trying to fit in everyone's boxes for us. And then we will tire, and realize we must begin again. We are running around our lives instead of standing in the middle of them.

So, *this*, my friends, is the work we are doing . . . whatever it takes to stay put and allow ourselves to be held.

This is the work we are doing . . . making the following our minute-by-minute mantra:

> We will not compare ourselves with each other as if one of us were better and another worse. We have far more interesting things to do with our lives. Each of us is an original. (Gal. 5:26)

• • •

God, in order to follow you and trust the work you are doing in my life, I may need to disappoint . . .

day 50 THE ONLY PERSON IN YOUR WAY IS YOU

The servant given one thousand said, "Master, I know you have high standards and hate careless ways, that you demand the best and make no allowances for error. I was afraid I might disappoint you, so I found a good hiding place and secured your money. Here it is, safe and sound down to the last cent."

The master was furious. "That's a terrible way to live!"

—Matthew 25:24–26

God has opened up spaces in my life. He has cleared a path for me and has provided opportunity. He's given me certain resources, talents. He's done that for you too. I can bury that opportunity out of fear that I'll mess it all up. Or, I can open my hands and give away what he's given to me.

I can practice expanding. Showing up. Using my voice. Trusting my instincts. Taking a risk. Making an investment . . . even if that investment is in me.

We do not take this on as a mantle of worry and fear and pressure bearing down on us. God's expectations of us are not crushing. He is not so much worried about outcomes as he is ownership. What irks him is when we bury what he's given us. When we find a good hiding place, thinking we're doing him a favor by protecting his investment. This was never the plan.

I secretly believed I would experience a level of approval that would confirm I was doing the right thing. Wouldn't that make it easy? An external confirmation that we're on the right track? I could just play small until that affirmation showed up, but God began surgically addressing my self-sabotage.

What do you want that you're afraid of having, Leeana?

The only person in your way, Leeana, is you. You are afraid that getting what you want will cost you what you have, and that feels like you are caught again. What if there is a third way that I could cut through the landscape of all this?

Ultimately, you need to confront your control. Once again, I'm asking you to stop running and turn and look at what you are so afraid of. Let's look at it for what it is. Again, the small injured part of you cannot withstand exposure. She is covering and hovering and posturing and she is so very worried about what everyone is thinking of her. She is aware of how many and whose eyes are on her. She is deeply self-conscious. She is deeply image-conscious. She is painfully, acutely aware of who is watching. This is something you can actually leave behind.

It's habit more than it's helpful.

You are in your own way, Leeana, and we have to confront that. In every place where you're blocking your own progress, we have to root that out. With compassion. And this is one of those places. Big-time. Do you feel your anxiety and hesitance and confusion and all the swirling? That's an indication you're afraid of getting what you really want.

Let's stop, and begin again.

Expansion is not about hustling our way out into the world, scratching and climbing out of an anxious need for upward mobility. Expansion is about our becoming. It is about God carving out a place for us in this world and us deciding we will step into that place. Wholeheartedly. Unapologetically.

• • •

> Some of us are only filling out about one-eighth of the space God has offered us in the world. Some of us are trying to fill out someone else's space. Some of us are refusing to set foot in the place he has made for us, because we are afraid of how we'll be perceived, afraid of failure, afraid of success, afraid God got it wrong this time.

What is God calling you to do? What investment is God calling you to make? What is holding you back from stepping into that space?

___

___

___

day 51 THE ALTAR

Then God said, "Take your son, your only son, whom you love—Isaac—and go to the region of Moriah. Sacrifice him there as a burnt offering on a mountain I will show you."

—Genesis 22:2 NIV

Surrender begets surrender, because we see—once we tolerate the invitation—that giving God the most precious, precarious parts of our lives is in our best interest.

Everything we are, everything we have, God has given to us. Freely and without strings attached. We get to do with it whatever we want. Our gifts, our relationships, our callings, our time, our resources, our very breath. Is God asking us to put a knife to the throat of all we love? Not literally, no. But over and over and over again he asks us to give back to him, open up, so that he can give us more.

When God stops Abraham's hand from injuring Isaac, he also tells Abraham that he will give him descendants that outnumber the stars in the sky, the grains of sand on the beach. When Abraham chooses to give back to God that which is most precious to him, his hands are then open to receive more.

Is God inviting you toward what you perceive to be a wall, an ending? If so, could you hold space for the possibility that this wall may, on closer inspection, become a door into all of eternity—something bigger and more transcendent than you can imagine?

> You're blessed when you stay on course,
> walking steadily on the road revealed by GOD. (Ps. 119:1)

Beginning again—whether in the smallest moment or the largest—usually requires us to put something on the altar. Our ego. Our resentments. Our regrets. Our anger. Our fear. Our dreams. Our past, present, future. Our beloveds. Most of all, perhaps, beginning again requires that we put our narratives of scarcity on the altar. We get stuck because we refuse to believe in the reality of abundance or the possibility that abundance could be for us and not just for everyone else.

Beginning again—whether in the smallest moment or the largest—usually requires us to put something on the altar.

The mark of beginning-again spirituality is abundance. We surrender because we trust, somewhere deep down, that God is a giver and not just a taker. He has more—not less—for us.

Yes, maybe God is asking you to place something unthinkably precious on the altar. But like the cross, the altar isn't the final resting place of the story.

Life, new life, is the story. What we thought was a wall might be a door . . . is the story. Beginning again, especially after the darkness of death . . . is the story. Because what is waiting for us, if we will moment by moment believe, is more.

And to those of us who cannot, yet, put our scarcity on the altar and give it back to God, we are as loved and as held as ever. He will always be inviting us to Moriah, up the mountain, so that he can provide a ram in the thicket and make good on promises galore. But if we cannot go, if we cannot climb, if we cannot stack the sticks or strike the flint, he will not curse us.

And yet, he will never stop calling.

Always, though, we get to decide. Will we clutch, self-protect, control? Or will we give back to God what we have—however beautiful or broken—so that he might be able to fill the sky of our lives with something we cannot yet see?

• • •

What keeps you from opening your hands to God?

God, if I surrender this precious part of my life to you,
I'm afraid . . .

____

____

____

day 52 CHECKING OUT VERSUS REAL REST

It's useless to rise early and go to bed late,
and work your worried fingers to the bone.
Don't you know he enjoys
giving rest to those he loves?

—*Psalm 127:2*

When my twins were first born, and they would miraculously nap simultaneously, I would lie down on the couch with a spoonful of peanut butter in one hand and a Diet Coke in the other and watch reruns of *Dawson's Creek*.

I was in what one might call Survival Mode, and all I could manage was checking out. I don't think this is necessarily evil. I've just come to realize that checking out is not the same thing as real, restorative rest. Real rest brings us back to our center, while checking out takes us far away from ourselves.

Real rest is hard to come by, though, isn't it? Just today I was being shot in the back of the leg with a Nerf gun while another child was licking my arm. When life gets overwhelming, all you want to do is *run* to your phone and start lapping up Instagram like it's your next meal.

But at some point, we need to exit Survival Mode—even if it's for an hour or two a week—and learn how to practice the kind of rest that brings us back to ourselves and back to the moment instead of taking us out to sea.

What this has meant for me is relearning what is actually restful to me, and then incorporating those resting practices into my life more regularly. Create a rhythm, so to speak.

Nurturing a healthy life rhythm is about beginning a dialogue with yourself that includes grace, compassion, and a sense of humor instead of the usual ways we deal with ourselves (i.e., contempt, frustration, and disappointment).

This is the kind of conversation you might have with a dear friend. Non-judgy, but genuinely supportive. Except that you're having it with yourself. Because *you are* the dear friend *to you*. (Revolutionary.)

You might say to yourself, "What would you like to do if you had three hours to yourself? What would be fun, delightful, freeing?"

or

"What do you need today, love? What does your body need? What does your soul need?"

Then take notes for yourself. Because you are that kind of friend.

• • •

List some ideas for:

Daily rest

Weekly rest

Monthly rest

Quarterly rest

Annual rest

day 53 SCOUTING BEAUTY

The sweetest thing in all my life has been the longing . . . to find the place where all the beauty came from.

—C. S. Lewis

Regular doses of natural beauty is one of my most essential rituals of rest. Because I've learned this about myself, I pay attention now.

For example: I hadn't seen fireflies in at least two decades, and then just a few weekends ago I was at a cabin in central Virginia, and as twilight descended, tiny Edison bulbs flickered against the fishing pond and the forested gravel road. This is so entirely unlike where I am from, Southern California, where headlights and neon signs replace fireflies.

But there they were, flickering, flirting with us. *Catch me if you can.* My kids could grab them out of the air and watch them inside cupped hands. As night fell, I saw the absolute magic of light flickering, even for a second, in the dark.

The humid air was thick on our skin and in our lungs, and a croaking frog sounded deeply distressed from his place on the pond bank. The twilight world was loud with life. But all eyes were on the fireflies.

Luke emptied the last of the gallon jug of orange juice into a cup and all eight cousins went about making a habitat. They poked holes in the plastic jug, collected leaves and rocks and sticks. They caught fireflies with their bare hands and deposited them in the jug. Then they shook the jug slightly. Just to jostle the creatures. And the jug lit up like a homemade flashlight.

"It's bioluminescence," Lane said.

She was right, of course—a chemical reaction happening inside those tiny bugs that made them shine. Each time a cousin agitated the orange juice jug, the lights came on.

Each night we waited and waited for enough darkness to descend so that we could see the tiny lanterns floating around us. Each night they did, and it was the most incredible thing I had ever seen.

• • •

What is something beautiful you've seen recently?

day 54 WHY AM I STRUGGLING IF THIS IS WHAT I'VE ALWAYS WANTED?

God has come to help his people.

—Luke 7:16 NIV

The human body's urge to breathe is irrepressible and essential. When we hold our breath, we begin to feel a pain inside our chest. This is called our critical line, a signal it's time for another breath. Everyone's critical line is different, but everyone—at some point—must breathe.

Research shows we hit our critical line not necessarily because our body needs oxygen, but because our body needs to release carbon dioxide. When we hold our breath, our body tells us it's time to exhale. Only then can we take in the air we need.

"As it turns out," a breathing researcher writes, "the opposite of holding your breath isn't inhaling, it's letting go."[1]

Between the years of 2008 and 2012—which included the birth of my first children (boy/girl twins), the challenges of learning to be a working writer, two moves within my hometown of San Diego, a miscarriage, another pregnancy, a move to the Middle East for my husband's job in the Navy, the birth of our third child in the Middle East, and a move back to San Diego with three small children in tow—I went through a bit of a Come Apart. Or, to say it in breathing terms, I hit my critical line.

I had been holding my breath for years—probably more years than I realized—trying to manage the pain in my chest. Trying to stave off surrender. Trying to keep it all together.

Until I couldn't anymore.

This is not to say that those four years were horrible. They absolutely were not. In most every way, they were some of the richest, most textured years I've lived. Which is why things got so very confusing. If life was so beautiful (and it was) and I had so much to be grateful for (and I did), why was I struggling? Why did I feel like I was being squeezed relentlessly? Why did everything feel so urgent? So suffocating? All the time?

Sure, we had stress. No one would deny that. But our life wasn't coming apart, not in the ways you think of someone's life crumbling. If anything, our life was arriving, precious dose after precious dose.

Still, I could not breathe.

My inability to suck it up and manage, let alone celebrate my life, exposed and highlighted my growing suspicion that I was grossly inadequate for my own life. I begrudged my critical line and believed something was wrong with me because I couldn't just push past it like it seemed so many others were able to do, like I had always been able to do.

My refusal to exhale, to let go, just about drowned me.

So I started reading literature from the 12-step program Emotions Anonymous, because I knew 12-step helped people break down something that had become unmanageable. In the Emotions Anonymous materials, I read a sentence that changed everything for me. It said,

We do not deserve to keep hurting ourselves.

Like a film sequence, I saw myself in a closed loop that I couldn't exit: struggle, self-contempt, swirling . . . struggle, self-contempt, swirling . . .

Why can't I just get it together? Why can't I just make it all look like she does over there? Why am I struggling when this is what I've always wanted?

I needed someone or something to release the valve on the blood pressure cuff that was squeezing my soul. I needed the anxious intensity to dissipate. I needed a place I could go where no one would try to convince me of how blessed I am or how I should simply pray harder. I needed people and words and spaces that were filled with grace, that honored my struggle. I needed someone to give me permission to exhale, because I could not offer it to myself.

• • •

Has there been a time in your life when you hit your critical line? Write about what that was like. Or if you are there now, write about what you're currently experiencing.

____

____

____

____

____

What helps you exhale?

____

____

____

____

____

day 55 THE WORN PATH

Lost, all lost in wonder at the God thou art.
—Saint Thomas Aquinas

We never get over being human. We don't arrive. We don't reach mastery. We don't graduate in any way. We show up and participate day after day. Returning. Re-praying. Re-creating. Re-loving. Re-celebrating. Re-listening. Re-forgiving. Re-resting. Re-abstaining. Re-grieving. Re-breathing.

The secret is to get up every morning and, with intention, step into the broad grace we have been offered for this mercies-are-new day. And then do it again tomorrow.

Like a ritual.
Like a practice.
Like recovery.

That's the only answer.

We get well by taking the small steps toward getting well. We learn to breathe by breathing. We learn to pray by praying. We learn to forgive by forgiving. We learn to accept by accepting. The miracle is in the one-foot-in-front-of-the-other participation.

If today, if this hour, if this year has not been what you had hoped, you can begin again. And in fact, if today, if this hour, if this year was perfect, you still—must—begin again. We must wake up and choose to live in each minute, each day, each year. Moment by moment. Beginning again.

We must choose to love, to create, to breathe, to return, to quiet down, to believe. Over and over again.

We must choose to love, to create, to breathe, to return, to quiet down, to believe. Over and over again.

One of the most revolutionary things we can do is allow those around us to begin again. And, of course, allow ourselves. None of this is easy.

I'm in "baby step" land altogether too much, forgetting what I've already learned a thousand times.

So I blow it. I mess up big-time. I feed the hungry grudge that's growing inside me. I nourish my rights to an easier day, an easier life.

And then I imagine a gentle monk whispering these words to me: "Oh, Leeana. You are a child of God. Always we begin again."

I bow my head and say, *Here I am again, God, walking the worn path of need. Walking the worn path of your love. See you again tomorrow. Amen.*

• • •

God, Today I need you because . . .

day 56 FROM VOID TO VALIDATION

But me he caught—reached all the way
from sky to sea; he pulled me out
Of that ocean of hate, that enemy chaos,
the void in which I was drowning.
They hit me when I was down,
but God stuck by me.
He stood me up on a wide-open field;
I stood there saved—surprised to be loved!

—Psalm 18:16–19

About a year ago, our church offices caught fire when a faulty copy machine shorted. The fire started around 4:00 a.m., so no one was injured, but the majority of the office space was a black crisp when the staff arrived to inspect the aftermath. One million dollars' worth of damage.

One of the pastors brought in a therapist to facilitate a conversation around the staff's experience of the fire, an opportunity to debrief. The therapist explained that some staff members might register the fire as an inconvenience, even a loss, while other staff members would internalize the fire as a trauma.

Trauma to one person isn't necessarily trauma to another, which is awfully confusing. How we internalize current life events is largely related to how we've internalized and flushed out past life events. If we've got big experiences stuck inside us, then current experiences will likely trigger those we're already carrying.

Feelings and experiences don't translate the same for everyone.

What's hard about this is that we tend to look for validation from those around us, permission to feel what we're feeling. And so many of us have been told that what we're feeling just can't be right.

Because so many others have it so much worse, what I'm up against doesn't get to be difficult.

Some of us lived in families where we were literally not allowed to have our own reactions to events. Some of us believe God would be disappointed if we struggled. Some of us will only ever feel what everyone else in the room is feeling because we would never trust that our own intuition or instinct could be valid.

We've let others talk us out of our experiences. We've let our ideas of God talk us out of our experiences. And we've talked ourselves out of our experiences.

But this is a way we hurt ourselves—denying our truth. And as 12-step tells us, "We do not deserve to keep hurting ourselves." When we refuse to validate our struggles, we are not only hurting ourselves, we are also drowning in a void, to take a line from Psalm 18.

Drowning in a void. Doesn't that say it all? God knows we don't just drown in circumstances and crises. We drown in our own refusal to acknowledge and validate our struggle. We drown in toxic thinking. We drown in internal chaos. That void can be just as dangerous and deadly as any catastrophe.

Just as the psalmist did, I believe we have been offered a salvation, a hand reaching down to pull us out of the void and deliver us into a spacious place, a wide-open field, an expanse. From void to validation, surprised to be so loved.

That's the whole story.

• • •

Is there a struggle you are currently experiencing that you are spending time and energy trying to talk yourself out of because it does not feel "worthy"? Write it out below.

Currently I am struggling with . . .

____

____

____

____

____

day 57 WARRIOR SISTERS

When we honestly ask ourselves which person
in our lives means the most to us, we often find
that it is those who, instead of giving advice, solutions,
or cures, have chosen rather to share our pain and touch
our wounds with a warm and tender hand.

—Henri Nouwen

Let's say yes and thank you to all the women who have taken our babies out of our arms when they see us, who wipe down our kitchen counters, who help us at the park when we can't manage all the kids, who feed our kids because their snacks are always better, who coax us out for nights on the town, who let us see their messes, who see ours.

When we feel as exposed and vulnerable as we have ever felt, you are gentle.

When we are manic and panicked and pinging off the walls, talking way too fast, and spinning stories about ourselves that don't hold up, you tell us we're OK, we're doing great, life is difficult and we're pulling it off, and that—just perhaps—we might want to limit our caffeine intake ever so slightly.

Let's say yes and thank you to the extraordinary true beauties in our lives, the Warrior Sisters, who have inched their way in with great care.

They put us on the stretcher and cut a hole in the roof where Jesus is and lower us down. Herky-jerky with sawdust in our hair, singing show tunes and complimenting us on our outfit, feeding us and praying for us.

These Warriors get us to Jesus. They take us by the hand and help us walk—one step at a time—into whatever life presents.

They surround us like a herd of mama elephants, protecting one of their own during childbirth, and they stamp the ground and stir up the dust and raise their trunks on our behalf.

They keep vigil. Stand watch. Pray. Light candles. Group text. Hold hope. Send memes. They raise their swords. They laugh and they cry and they sit and rub our back and do not say a single word.

Sometimes I'm scared to let the Warrior Sisters in my life see me. Maybe you've been hurt at the hands of other women in the past, and it's easy to believe that because one person hurt you, everyone will. Could you let these Warrior Sisters inch closer to you? Could you open up a bit more? Could you let God love you through them? When I do, I am always anchored and winged. I am always a better me.

• • •

Who are your Warrior Sisters?

____

____

____

Who can you be a Warrior Sister to?

____

____

____

day 58 WE ARE ALL HEARTBROKEN

The more we are able to embrace our sorrow and learn from it,
the more we will also be capable of experiencing great joy.
Yet to embrace our sorrow takes a great deal of courage.
So often we try to soften or resist our pain.

—Emotions Anonymous

I once heard educator and activist Parker Palmer say, "We are all heartbroken." He went so far as to say, the one thing he and the terrorists who drove planes into buildings on September 11, 2001, have in common is that "we are all heartbroken."

Well, except me, Parker Palmer. I'm not heartbroken. Good Christians aren't heartbroken. Mothers of three aren't heartbroken. Blessed blondes like me aren't heartbroken. You must be mistaken on that one. I'm just over here pulling up a chair to my refrigerator. Heartbroken, you say?

Naaaaaah. Not me.

This is what I want to say. What I want to feel. What I wish were true. Some of us learned along the way that our pain is an inconvenience to others and probably to God too. We've also learned that faithful people don't come apart. Faithful people are stable.

We've also feared that if we turn toward that ache for even one moment, it will swallow us whole. So we turn the other way—away from our own need—and we send the message to ourselves, countless times, that what's hurting us isn't reasonable. We've gagged the ache with Doritos and Diet Coke. We've covered it up with bronzer. We've smothered it with layers and layers of trying-too-hard. We've shut it up with the how-richly-blessed-we-are talk.

You don't need anyone to cosign on a Come Apart. In other words, you don't need to wait until someone else tells you that your particular struggle is worthy enough to call life hard. If it feels hard, then it's hard. If you're lost, it's OK to say it.

To not say it, I've found, is one of the most flagrant and egregious ways we hurt ourselves.

. . .

God, I am admitting that I am absolutely heartbroken about . . .

____

____

____

____

____

God, what do you want to say to me about my heartbreak?

day 59 BREATHING ROOM

When we're carrying unattended ache,
we have to work to keep ahead of it.
—*from* Breathing Room

Breathing room is available when—and only when—we face the very thing we don't want to face.

We decide to no longer dismiss or override what we are feeling because doing so is a personal abandonment, a betrayal. We know it's not OK to bully other people, but somehow we forgot—or never learned—that it's not OK to bully ourselves.

How do we find the spacious place? The place where we accept ourselves—forgive ourselves, even? The place where we live with the profound sense that we are loved? How do we find our way to that place? To that person?

We begin right where we are. With the ugly truth. With the ache. We confess we cannot get ourselves up off the floor. We admit our self-contempt. And we invite Christ to come and sit with us, perhaps offering a snack if we have one to spare.

We don't stay in the ache forever, of course. That would be *despair*. But we can't avoid the struggle either. That would be *denial*. We have to turn toward the ache with even the tiniest *desire* to get well.

"There is a hole in your being," Henri Nouwen says, "like an abyss. You will never succeed in filling that hole because your needs are inexhaustible.

You have to work around it so that gradually the abyss closes. Since the hole is so enormous and your anguish so deep, you will always be tempted to flee from it. There are two extremes to avoid: being completely absorbed in your pain and being distracted by so many things that you stay far away from the wound you want to heal."[1]

I begin to practice what it feels like to offer up my pain, because I could see the more I denied it, the more it controlled me. I begin to work around the abyss with a confession, a stripped-down utterance of inconvenient truth. That's how things begin to change, I've learned. By standing toe-to-toe with the truth.

We do not live in denial.
We do not live in despair.
We live into the desire to get well.

• • •

Are you currently experiencing denial, despair, or desire?
Write a bit about that.

___

___

___

day 60 THIS IS NOT AN URGENT MATTER

God, grant me the serenity to accept the things I cannot change; the courage to change the things I can; and the wisdom to know the difference.

—The Serenity Prayer

Recently I received something that made me feel very, very defensive. Has this ever happened to you? You immediately begin swirling, thinking through all the ways you could and should mount a bulletproof defense.

I lurched into fix-it mode, frantic to exonerate myself, frantic to prove that in fact I was the one everyone should be listening to.

My friend Tina called me, and I told her the whole story. What I had received. How it made me feel. Talking one million miles an hour.

Tina calmly said, "This is not an urgent matter. No matter what it feels like, Leeana, this is not an urgent matter." She said a lot of other really smart things in that conversation too, but what I held in my head as a mantra was, "This is not an urgent matter."

How many times do we pick up something, assuming it's urgent, and take on the fixing of it when we never needed to grab it in the first place?

"Working hard and working out of a place of anxiety are not the same thing," my spiritual director, Beth, tells me. "If you can't breathe, stop. Never move or act out of that place. Wait until you can breathe."

In other words, ignore that impulse to make it all so urgent. Just flat-out ignore it. Do the exact opposite of what that anxious defensiveness is convincing you that you must do. The. Exact. Opposite. Just be still.

Trying to defend myself, trying to fix this perceived problem, was doomed. All I was going to do by jumping into action was make it worse. I can see that now. In the moment, though, it felt like I would suffocate if I didn't solve, solve, solve.

So on that particular day, I did the exact thing I did not want to do: I did nothing. And it was the best possible nonurgent decision I could have ever made.

• • •

What feels urgent right now that may not actually be?

day 61 HEALING INSTEAD OF FIXING

When Jesus saw him lying there and learned that he had been in this condition for a long time, he asked him, "Do you want to get well?"

—John 5:6 NIV

Most every writer I love is a recovering addict of some kind.

Here's my theory on recovering addicts, those who are actually staying sober: they've got a few secrets the rest of us don't.

First, they get, in a really profound way, that pretending is not something to be celebrated. I think this is actually revolutionary, and I also think most of us have no idea how to live this way.

Second, they understand we are recovering, always, and not recovered. Every day they have to nurture their sobriety. It's not something automatic. Even after years and years. They have to get up with intention for today. They have to begin again.

Third, if you're a recovering addict, somehow—strangely—I believe you are learning how to have the right perspective of yourself. That you are both in need of grace and worthy of grace. That you are both a mess and a miracle. The rest of us are still trying to figure this out.

Fourth, recovering addicts have taken steps to pursue their own healing and yet know they are not responsible for healing themselves.

They have admitted to themselves that something in their life became unmanageable, which I believe is an extraordinarily courageous thing to do. Something we probably all need to do, if you ask me.

At this point in my life, when I'm over the easy-come, easy-go answers and the dangerous notion that if we just look at something long enough, we'll be able to simply fix it once and for all, I'm drawn to people who aren't trying to fix everyone else and, instead, are really serious about getting well themselves.

This nonfixing posture agrees with my spirit.

I've been thinking about the difference between fixing and healing. Fixing is a solution, while healing is a process. Jesus healed in the New Testament.

Sometimes in one shebang. But always with a person's process in mind. Not to wield control, but to whisper compassion. To show them the path of life instead of death, inviting them to participate in their own lives: "Do you want to get well?" he asks.

Fixing allows us to stay in control, which will never, ever work. We get to call the shots instead of having to truly and deeply relinquish. Fixing is our way of saying, I want to feel better, instead of, I want to get better.

Most of us know there's something inside us we need to face. We just need to get brave enough to let it rise up to the top. It's tied down in the deeper waters, waiting for us to cut it loose.

• • •

Think about a time in your life when you tried to fix something. Now think about a time in your life when you went through a season of healing. What was the difference between the two?

day 62 BORROWED PRAYERS

i who have died am alive again today . . .
(now the ears of my ears awake and
now the eyes of my eyes are opened)

—e. e. cummings

During internally intense seasons of life, I've had to completely relearn how to pray. When things have become difficult and my capacity for BS diminished, I find it practically impossible to turn to God and pretend. So there have been seasons when nothing came out.

The poet Carrie Fountain writes about prayer, "I practiced rigorously. Just as I was getting good, I lost it."[1]

Unintentionally, I think we turn the sacred into something to get good at, a skill. Like tennis. Or chess. Or baking. And somehow, prayer gets lumped in with that must-master mentality. Then we see—we learn through our desperation—that prayer is much more about being human than being holy.

There was a time I could not find a single word for God that felt true. Perhaps this meant that somewhere inside I was angry that God had allowed the Hard. I felt betrayed a bit, by him, by life.

Has this ever happened to you? You just can't seem to find any kind of words that actually put sentiment to what you're experiencing. Everything that was ever said feels hollow, like a dumb joke on a greeting card. Like piety instead of a plea.

I had completely forgotten the insight of Thomas Merton and Saint Augustine: that the very desire to pray can be our most meaningful prayer. I had forgotten that prayer, like everything else in life, wasn't about my performance as much as my posture. I had forgotten that just turning my heart toward God in the desperation I felt was so much more important than any particular words I could manufacture.

And yet, I wanted words too, which isn't so wrong. It's OK to want to be able to put words to the chaos and give those words over as an offering. I wanted God to turn them over in his hands and send them back to me, collected, categorized, organized. Fixed.

None of this happened, of course. The words were not in me. Or maybe they were, but they were so buried, and I did not have the spiritual pickaxe needed to unearth and excavate.

I decided to hold out for true words instead of bullying myself into praying words I didn't believe or feel. Forcing ourselves to be false, especially to God, is a way we abandon ourselves. I needed to give myself permission to fall silent for a time until I could be truly honest.

I needed to give myself permission to fall silent for a time until I could be truly honest.

In my silence, the words of e. e. cummings's poem "i thank You God for most this amazing" kept floating by: "i who have died am alive again today."[2]

These words must have come to me intuitively, dare I say even prophetically. They articulated what I wanted so deeply though I couldn't find my own words to say. I wanted to be alive again today, to be awake and open to the world, to feel amazed and thankful, to feel the sun. I wanted to be able to feel the gratitude I knew was inside me somewhere.

When these words came to me, I prayed them. I would offer them, unedited, on faith that they were saying something for me I couldn't say for myself.

Of course, this is nothing new. The tradition of praying others' words, specifically the words of Scripture, has been around since the third century when the scholar Origen began to teach "Scripture as sacrament." His ideas later led to Saint Benedict's establishment of Lectio Divina as a monastic practice in the sixth century.

Borrowing the words of Scripture and meditating on them was a way to experience Scripture as Living Word, finding truth for today in ancient words.

Do you need to begin again with some of your faith practices? I think this is more than OK. Resize and reshape your conversations with God—whatever it takes to keep returning.

...

Describe your current relationship with prayer.

---

day 63 GOD IN A BOX

You are imperfect, you are wired for struggle, but you are worthy of love and belonging.

—Brené Brown

The times when we have the least capacity to let others in are precisely the times when we need to open ourselves up the most. This is so hard. I'm the kind of person who, if I'm honest, would prefer control over help. But, I'm learning, I don't always get to be in control. And when the chaos enters, I better let myself spill open just a tad, so that the comfort can enter too.

I remember a particularly lonely season in my life. I was separated from all my friends, living on the other side of the world. I believed God wanted to keep me company; I just didn't know how. But I prayed for space so he could show me.

Three days later, I received a box in the mail from a handful of my dearest friends back in San Diego. The customs form on this box should have read "Detailed list of contents: love." Notes scrawled on napkins and Post-its, gifts for my children, perfectly pale pink nail polish, mix CDs, magazines, snacks from Target, sour candy.

I immediately realized Emmanuel, the Company Keeper, had come to me in a cardboard box. Christ in the bread and wine of Sour Patch Kids, the sacrament of Archer Farms Tex Mex mix.

Christ scrawled on napkins. Christ in love notes on Post-its.

Who says you can't put God in a box.

These Warrior Sisters reached all the way across oceans to hold on to me, which feels so radical in its generosity and acceptance.

Letting others in is a better way to live, even though it requires bringing down our defenses and allowing for the possibility that being seen and being known might be more meaningful than being in control.

In some ways, it's simpler to keep people at arm's length. Much less complicated. But then there are those times when we are reduced and at our end and someone sends us a box that says "I see you. I hear you. I love you," and the grace of being witnessed in our struggle is the very thing that gets us through.

I am jittery and nuts most of the time, and I worry—so deeply—that people will get to a part of me that somehow will no longer work for them. I worry that people will want too much from me, more than I can give. I worry that there will be a cost to letting others in, more than I can pay.

But you know what? It never works to isolate, to pretend, to shut down. It never works to try to be the one in control all the time. It never works to try to carry all of life's burdens alone.

I see how Christ has helped me feel found through these women. It all begins by letting them in.

• • •

Was there a time when you let someone in to your life and you got burned? Has that experience kept you from letting others in?

What does God want to say to you about letting others in to your life?

day 64 PRACTICING MY HUMANITY

The Higher Power's plans are far superior to anything that my manipulating and scheming could bring about. What a relief not to be God!

—*Emotions Anonymous*

I sit at the master bedroom window, behind my $30 turquoise desk, staring at our surroundings. I watch the wind lift the skirts of the trees. I watch the wind create a symphony of rustling palm fronds that builds and wanes like strings. I watch the wind carry blue jays and orioles. I watch the wind pull and push streaks of clouds.

I want to be the wind. Light. Carefree. Breathless in its wandering.

I want to be the wind. The force that controls and moves. I want to be the Source. In charge of blowing things where I choose. Scattering when I want. Pushing doors open. Blowing down barriers.

I want to be the wind. I want to be the god. The brawn. The life. The power. The mover. The shaker. The beauty-maker.

I confess: I want to be the wind. But all my huffing and puffing just makes my soul asthmatic.

> The Spirit of life in Christ, like a strong wind, has magnificently cleared the air, freeing you from a fated lifetime of brutal tyranny at the hands of sin and death. (Rom. 8:2)

God is the wind. I am the woman. God is the God. I am the human. When I practice being not God—nonGodly—I am trusting God's God-ness.

The truth is, I'm not always sure I can trust what he's doing. I'm not always sure I can trust that he will bring things to an acceptable resolution. I'm not always sure I can trust him with those I love. I'm not always sure I can trust him to fix the mess I'm staring at.

But I want to, and I believe that matters.

So I just keep asking God to help me stop strangling my own life and the lives of everyone else I love, and let him be the strong God-wind. I ask God to help me forgive myself for being human. And I ask God to help me accept (which is the last stage of grief, incidentally) my role and his role in this crazy world.

• • •

Where are you reaching for control? In what situation, relationship, endeavor?

____

____

____

Where are you wanting to be God?

What does it mean to be human in this situation?

day 65 WHAT HAS CHRIST ASKED YOU TO CARRY?

Here is a boy with five small barley loaves and two small fish, but how far will they go among so many?

—John 6:9 NIV

I am forever juggling one too many objects at any given time in my day. Cell phone, car keys, ID, purse, beverage (always, always a beverage or even *two*), some toy-of-the-hour that each kid must have before leaving the house.

Something hanging from every finger. Jackets clenched under each arm. My ID between my teeth. My cell phone wedged between my chin and chest. My coffee mug squeezed between elbow and side. Two backpacks and a purse on one shoulder. All this while trying to hold hands through the parking lot or herd kids safely across the street.

Without fail, something falls.

I drop the cell phone and the case explodes. The ID falls out of my teeth and into the gutter. The purse comes careening off my shoulder and lands with a thud on my crooked elbow, causing the coffee to splash out of the mug and onto my shoes. The car keys—every single time—try to escape.

It's like the Tankersley Circus has come to town day after day after day.

If I were watching myself go by, I'd say, *Why doesn't she just carry less?* I want the courage to be un-frantic, to be un-frenzied, to be un-fidgety, to let go of all the desperation. I want to stop buying into the lie that it's all so urgent, that things will invariably fall apart if I'm not the one jumping in and holding them all together.

What happens when we try to keep control of everything? Something drops. Then something else. Our own health is damaged. A relationship we care about is damaged. Our capacity to really enjoy our life is damaged. In the end, the people around us become resentful because they never asked us to be the savior of the universe. They just asked us to be present with them, breathing next to them, playing cards or having a snack with them.

I look to Christ who, last time I checked, has not asked me to do his job for him. What has Christ asked me to carry? If I'm honest, very little. In fact, if anything, over and over, he asks me to hand him anything I believe I possess.

He says, *Bring me your five loaves and two fish. Let me feed the crowds with your crumbs.* The very act of letting go of our lunch is a powerful reminder of our humanity, our meanness, our tendency for defensiveness and anxious activating. We want to be the ones who know better, who feed the crowds, and we want the pleasure and satisfaction of everyone else seeing we know better too.

But this little plan—our Frantic Efforts to Appear Recovered—will only backfire. Making us more frantic, and more, and more, and more.

If our cell phones are shattered, our shoes are covered in coffee, and our pinky finger is broken from carrying a twenty-pound purse, I wonder what our souls look like. I wonder what our relationships look like.

We listen by stopping. No more striving. We acknowledge we've hit our critical line, yet again. In the stillness we exhale, asking God to show us why we're running so hard, juggling so frantically, just sure we have to fix everything. We let go with a long, forceful exhale so we can get what our soul really needs on the inhale: space, love, broad grace, therapy.

Christ says, *Bring me the stale saltines. Bring me the sardine carcass. Bring me the meager, the humble, the modest. That little old lunch. And watch me be God. Watch me set a table of glory. You show up, and let me show off.*

What's cool is that God comes through. He makes weird little miracles happen—the kind of thing I could never dream up or manufacture. God multiplies when all I can see is division. So that's where I'm putting my money today. I'm believing that God will make a mighty meal where I could have only created a peasant's rations.

• • •

God, I need to stop carrying . . .

____

____

____

day 66 MAKING AMENDS WITH MYSELF

When I am gentle with myself, I become gentle with others. It is this gentleness and caring, not impatience and criticism, which brings about continued growth and healing.

—Emotions Anonymous

Making amends is an idea popularized by the 9th step of the 12-step program. Making amends is about reaching out to those who have been injured in some way by our behavior and trying to restore what we have wrecked.

Amends is different from an apology.

An apology says, "I know I stole money from our family savings account in order to gamble, and I'm sorry." Amends says, "I know I stole money from our family savings account in order to gamble, and I've taken on a second job to pay that money back." Amends is not just words; it's engaging in restorative actions whenever possible. It's also a change in behavior.

In the 8th step, we are invited to make a list of all the persons we have harmed. What happens, so very often, is that our own name shows up somewhere on that list. Sometimes, right at the top.

We're beginning to see just how long we have been in the ring with ourselves. Our self-pity has kept us planted on the couch. Our worry has robbed us from experiencing pleasure. Our anger or rigidity at others mirrors the anger and rigidity we feel toward ourselves. Our need to please others has driven us to bully ourselves.

Freedom means "we're not ruled or held captive by any one part of us."[1]

One of the common methods for making amends is writing the offended party a letter. Soon after my third child was born, I decided, as a gesture of grace and acceptance, to write a letter of amends to myself.

Before I wrote the letter, I thought about sitting with a very kind and funny and gentle eighty-year-old version of myself. I asked what she'd tell me. I tried to connect with that deeper, more soulful version of me, the one with huge rings and a flowy caftan and lines on her face and a big smile. She reaches toward me, taking my hand, and says, I will show you the way.

• • •

Write a letter of amends to yourself.

Dear ____________________,

____

____

____

____

____

day 67 DESIRE IS A TRICKY THING

All my longings lie open before you, Lord;
my sighing is not hidden from you.
—Psalm 38:9 NIV

Desire is a tricky thing. We often skirt around it in lieu of what we "should" do, what we "need" to do, what we "must" do, even. We are skilled in the art of finding reasons why what we really want isn't actually what we really want and explaining away our heart's beat.

Mainly, I think, because heartbrokenness is hard. And when we name something we really want and then it doesn't happen—well, that's the best recipe I know for getting your heart broken.

So we do this thing, this safe thing. We abdicate our desires. We relinquish, resign, step down from, hand over, give up, abandon. I've done this before. I've decided to let someone else—someone who is much more productive or efficient or attractive or articulate or successful or whatever—handle it. I've avoided the fray for fear of heartbrokenness. But you know, I never save myself any trouble by abdicating my desires. I never find that approach more fulfilling.

I believe that dismissing what I really want (but believe I can't have or don't deserve or someone else got first) will make me feel better. What ends up happening is that I feel like I can't breathe. I feel like I've lost the beat. I feel like I let a small piece of myself die for safety's sake. I've turned away from the Soul Voice, the longing, and I've told it to hush up—that it's not helpful or wanted.

I'm not talking about indulging our every whim. No, not at all. In fact, that's the opposite of what I'm talking about. This is not about our appetites, which are frivolous and even, sometimes, careless.

Our appetites are demanding and childish and usually leave us feeling worse for having them. At their best, our appetites are a manifestation of something deeper, some hunger we're longing to fill.

If we mix up appetites and desires—by overindulging our appetites or by depriving our desires—we will live hungry. In fact, sometimes the best thing we can do is get help understanding our appetites so that we can more fully experience our true desires.

Our desires come from that voice deep down inside that is unique to you, that longs to be heard, that is whispering important secrets to you about what really matters. True, gut-level desire, something God has written on your very soul. When we treat this voice like a liability, we are shutting something down in ourselves that's very hard to revive.

• • •

God, what I truly desire is . . .

day 68 EITHER SUPERHUMAN OR SUBHUMAN

The serpent was clever, more clever
than any wild animal God had made.

—Genesis 3:1

At some point in my life, I got into this really crazy thinking that if I couldn't be more than human (hyper-productive, hyper-amazing, hyper-perfect), then I was decidedly less than human.

If I can't be superhuman, then I am subhuman.

This is what happened to Adam and Eve in the Garden. This is the age-old lie. The snake told them, "You can be like God." But when they ate the apple and tried to be like God (more than human), they realized their nakedness and felt great shame (less than human). Their only recourse was radical defendedness. In other words, hiding.

I've tried to outwit my own humanity, time and time again. All this trying and striving ever delivers is shame, the impulse to go into hiding behind our false competency.

The voice of shame is the voice of the serpent in the Garden: "You can be like God. You can know everything. You can be more than human. Just take the bait." This sounds great. I can be more than human? I can be like God? I can do it all? Well, sign me up!

And we give in to the first and the greatest temptation of all time: to blur the distinction between humanity and God. We believe those voices telling us we can be, must be, in perfect control. We believe we should be all-knowing, all-able. And if we can't do it all, then we end up feeling like we can't do anything. Neither of which is true.

The Soul Bullies are selling absolutes. They speak in once-and-for-alls. They allow no space for complexity, paradox, or both/and. Toxic lies force us into either/or. The Soul Bullies say, "You are so weak." And what's worse, in our attempts to outrun our shame we will become desperate to prove, with every bit of trying-hard we can, "No, I'm not. See, look, I'm strong. I'm strong. I'm strong."

What's far more true of all of us is that we are, actually, both weak and strong.

Because one little weakness immediately means deficiency.

What's far more true of all of us is that we are, actually, both weak and strong. We are God-image and we are human. We have within us the heavenly divine as well as the lowly dirt. We are magic and mundane, vulnerable and resilient.

This is life. It doubles back on itself and gives you mourning and dancing in practically the very same moment. Beauty and struggle coexist.

Let go of the lies on the exhale, so we can take in the truth on the inhale.

Some days, I just assume that because I feel inadequate as a mother and a writer and a human, it must be true. Final judgments are cast in my head, and I accept them. You know what's true? I am struggling and I am soulful. And both are beautiful.

How are you trying to be superhuman?

When do you feel subhuman?

day 69 COME TO ME

Are you tired? Worn out? Burned out on religion? Come to me. Get away with me and you'll recover your life. I'll show you how to take a real rest. Walk with me and work with me—watch how I do it. Learn the unforced rhythms of grace. I won't lay anything heavy or ill-fitting on you. Keep company with me and you'll learn to live freely and lightly.

—Matthew 11:28–30

When I realize it's one of those days when things are growing grimmer and grimier at my house and I want to take out my self-contempt on anything and everything in my path, I try to remind myself that this is part of living. The down days. I haven't failed because I'm struggling. I'm just struggling. So what do I need to do?

I need to turn to myself as a mother would her child.

I think about Lane coming into my room in the middle of the night, desperately trying to breathe after croup descended on her in her sleep without warning. I scoop her up and race to the emergency room, holding her hand while I drive, asking her to squeeze my hand when she sees a green light, squeeze my hand when she sees a red light. I run her inside, fevery and wheezing, and I get her care.

I don't scold her for being ill. I don't roll my eyes at the inconvenience. I don't say, "Can't you get it together, Lane? This is so like you. To need all this help." I help her. Because I'm her mother. Because she needs me. Because she is my very heart in a little-girl body. Because she can't breathe.

I must think of myself in those same terms. Not as an inconvenience, but both as a child who is in need, and also as the strong mother who holds her child close and protects her with unending compassion.

If I can't breathe, I need to get myself to the care that I need. As I would for my darling Lane. Period.

I can talk myself into "sucking it up" and "not making such a big deal out of everything." Sure. But if I stuff down all my need, I rob myself of receiving fierce gentleness. I miss the divine plea—Come to me, all you who are weary and burdened—to allow myself the dignity of rest and recovery.

• • •

In what ways are you both the young child who is in need and the strong mother who cares for her child?

____

____

____

____

____

day 70 YOU DON'T NEED TO BE REASONABLE

The best way out is always through.

—Robert Frost

My friend Rickelle lost her baby boy, Lake, when she was twenty-five weeks pregnant.

He was there. And then he was gone.

In the aftermath of such a trauma, Rickelle started planting in their backyard. She watered flowers, and she got a tiny orange kitten named Everett. She said, "I needed things to nurture. I longed for that baby; I was ready for him. So I needed something alive to take care of."

Rickelle wrote "I believe" on her hand every morning when she got out of bed. Between her kitten and garden caretaking, she went to the garage with a power sander and put a hoodie on and listened to reggae while she refinished furniture.

This just goes to show you that you don't need to be reasonable when you are grieving. She told me, "You just do whatever makes you feel an inch closer to putting one foot in front of the other."

Life wants us to turn the calendar page even when our souls want to stop and commemorate what is happening now. Life wants us to go to sleep and wake up and move on. The calendar is not conducive to our souls. The world is functioning in clock-time *chronos*, but our souls speak God-time *kairos*.

My instinct is to try to stay ahead of the grief, to march forward by the beat of *chronos*. I'm the kind of person who would rather be "doing fine, thanks" than falling apart. But I've seen that the comfort does not come to those intent on coping. The comfort arrives for those who are willing to spill open.

Scripture says, "Blessed are those who mourn, for they will be comforted" (Matt. 5:4 NIV).

If we will allow ourselves the time and space to mourn, we will be comforted. On the other hand, if we believe we must suck it up and cope and steel ourselves against the loss, the comfort will be much harder to come by.

I learned from Rickelle that physically mourning—sanding, and watering, and digging, and feeding—blesses you with comfort. The act of letting go delivers gifts of comfort that marching on never will.

We allow a meal to be delivered. We allow a friend to sit quietly next to us. We allow God to touch us.

The calendar will not serve me in matters of the soul. I don't need to assess how worthy or unworthy my losses are, how they do or don't stack up to someone else's plight.

My job is simply to allow myself to feel all the losses and not be in charge of forcing it all back together again.

• • •

Do you have a grief unobserved in your story? If so, what could you do physically to observe your loss?

day 71 LIFELINES

When Moses' arms grew tired, Aaron and Hur brought a stone for him to sit on, while they stood beside him and held up his arms, holding them steady until the sun went down.

—Exodus 17:12 GNT

"I've been praying for lifelines," a friend of mine shared with me.

She is the mother of three very young children, all born right in a row, one of whom doesn't really feel the need to sleep. She's needed some space, some breathing room, and she's prayed that God would show her how she might be saved. I find this to be such a courageous and inspirational prayer.

God threw her a lifeline in the form of a local MOPS group at a church less than a mile from her house. The funny thing is, she didn't really see herself as someone who "needed" MOPS. Until she went. And she realized that she was sitting at a table with eight other women who had prayed that same prayer, and God brought them all together.

Lifelines don't always arrive in the packages we had expected or planned. Often, the lifelines meet in a cafeteria with fluorescent lighting. They are almost always an invitation for us to accept our own neediness.

Here we are. All of us. In need. Pass the coffee, please.

Some of us are waiting until we have the energy, the resources, the space, the right words, or the time to reach out. This is a ruse. It's like saying you're going to get in shape a bit more before you hire that personal trainer you need. This is the kind of thinking that allows us to keep ourselves at a safe distance from support. This is what we call self-sabotage.

The etymology of *reach out* takes us back to roots meaning "to extend oneself" and "torture," as in the idea of putting one's body on the rack. Well, doesn't that say it all.

Reaching out—the whole point of it—is that we do it in our most blind, most lost, most wordless, most depleted moments. Even though it doesn't feel good. Even though it feels like we're really extending ourselves beyond what's comfortable, dislocating those safely intact joints. Even though it feels torturous to be in need yet again.

We practice asking for help over and over so that next time we don't wait so long to get it. We allow God to bring us the help in ways that we would not have planned or contrived. We find ourselves in a room full of women we don't know, and after about fifteen minutes we realize God had been saving us a seat.

Reaching out can look like a lot of different things. Reaching out to a trusted friend, someone who will listen instead of advise. Someone who will simply stay in the room and breathe instead of trying to fix it all for us.

Reaching out might mean picking up the thousand-pound phone and calling a professional. Someone who is trained in spiritual direction or therapy or trauma recovery or making people laugh.

Reaching out might mean calling your sponsor or Your Group.

Reaching out could be attending that class or workshop you've been avoiding, choosing to gain tools instead of ignoring the issue.

Reaching out might be turning toward Christ with a borrowed prayer.

Reaching out might be sending the following text: “Help. I’m scared. Pray for me today. I don’t believe anymore. I need you to believe for me.”

Reaching out is one moment that gives us something to build on, the moment that interrupts our toxic trajectory and creates a momentum of health.

Reaching out is a step toward rescue.

• • •

Write about a lifeline that has arrived in your life that didn’t necessarily come to you in the way you would’ve expected.

day 72 THINGS WON'T ALWAYS FEEL THE WAY THEY DO RIGHT NOW

We do not think ourselves into new ways of living,
we live ourselves into new ways of thinking.
—Father Richard Rohr

The smallest miracle happened. One that I can't totally account for except to say that Christ saves us when we cannot save ourselves. Christ comes and sits with us when we cannot get ourselves up off the floor. The ways he saves us, the ways he keeps us company, are somewhat of a mystery. He arrives, and that's all I know.

This time, hope arrived on the wings of these words: "Things won't always feel the way they do right now."

I just chose to believe that statement when I could believe little else. I chose to believe the scald I was feeling would let up at some point. I chose to believe that someway, somehow (though I didn't know when or how) it was all going to pass.

I wasn't in charge of anything other than the chanting. I would say it ritualistically to myself because I knew that if I could just hold that phrase in my head, the mantra would crowd out all the Soul Bullies vying for airtime, and the truth might be able to find its way from my head to my heart.

My job was to put the good words on repeat so the bad words couldn't compete.

Every time I began to feel the burn of the scald, I would say, "Things won't always feel the way they do right now." And somehow those words carried me through.

We all have rituals that help us get through our anxiety or our fear or our shame. Our rituals are what we use to cope, what we turn to for comfort when we start to feel the squeeze.

Sometimes our rituals are healthy. Sometimes they are harmful. We choose ruin or we choose recovery. I attached to this concept. I could see it in my own life. What do I do, where do I turn, on the down days. Or, as I've come to realize, the down hour—which is often butted up against some kind of moment of bliss only to have that gnawing settle in again.

Creating and turning to rituals that nourish us when we're experiencing a downturn is one of the ways we care for ourselves, one of the ways we begin again.

We ask Christ to be our Company Keeper while we wait. Maybe nothing changes "out there," but having a strategy for coping with the panic can certainly change things "in here."

Going through emotionally demanding seasons in life can throw us into semihysterics at times. Or, let's be honest, even full-blown hysterics. Some days can feel so incredibly inefficient that you just want to scream. *What have I done? How did I get here? Are we really starting all over . . . again?*

When navigating change, it's too easy for me to believe life will never feel right again, life will always feel as hard as it does in that very moment. This mindset keeps me stuck in perpetual hand-wringing, and I need a way to stop the toxic loop.

Here's how I do it: "Things won't always feel the way they do right now." On repeat.

• • •

Is there a word or phrase God has brought you in times of stress and disorientation that has been particularly helpful?

____

____

____

day 73 YOU ARE NOT WHERE YOU WERE

He gives strength to the faint
and strengthens the powerless.
—Isaiah 40:29 CSB

I was talking with the most stunning twentysomething woman the other day. She told me about the ongoing sexual abuse she experienced in her home. She told me about how she fled, and how she fears that no matter what she does, she will always be defined by the abuse.

When I look at her and listen to her, I see this extraordinary soul—someone who is getting herself the help she needs, investing in her own healing and recovery, taking herself out into nature to ingest beauty, putting on mascara.

Her insides feel raw and traumatized and overwhelmed. But what I see when I look at her and hear her story is pure, unmitigated resilience.

She is doing it. She is showing up. She is living. The waters of her life have been as dirty and disgusting as one could imagine. Undoubtedly, life would feel so much simpler to just give in to the beige constantly looming all around her. And yet there she is, as vibrant as she could be, even in the midst of all that sludge.

She still feels buried, like the power of it all will never lift, but I want to say to her with conviction, "You are not where you were. You are moving through this. Slowly, painfully, indirectly. You have to believe, you are not where you were."

Are you tempted to believe that you are where you've always been and all the time and attention you've given to listening to God in your life has been a waste?

Fix your eyes on someone you know who is making his or her way through a disaster. Look at them. Watch their resilience even in the midst of tragedy. That same spirit is in you too.

If you will keep walking *your* path, I promise you, you will not be where you once were.

• • •

God, I feel stuck. Please remind me I am not where I once was.

____

____

____

day 74 NO MORE BAD PANTS

I'm afraid that sometimes you'll play lonely games too.
Games you can't win 'cause you'll play against you.
—*Dr. Seuss*

After I delivered all my babies, I would be so anxious to get out of my maternity jeans and into regular jeans that I would squeeze and contort and pour myself into ill-fitting pants just to be able to say to myself that I did it. What always, always ended up happening was my mood worsened and worsened as the day wore on and my body began swelling and oozing out of every seam.

Sometime after I had Elle I was sitting in traffic in my car with too-tight jeans on and felt, with such visceral disgust, my postpartum stomach observably expanding—like dough rising—out the top of my jeans. I said out loud after getting home and running upstairs to the safety and loyalty of my Zella yoga pants, "That's it. No more Bad Pants."

What I see, what catches me every time I've ever done this, as I'm peeling off the pants, is the red indentations all over my legs and stomach. Like a body that's been surgically scored. Isn't it amazing what we will do at our own expense?

I've decided that even if I have to wear something with a stretch waist-band the rest of my life, I'm not going to demean myself by wearing clothes that hurt me. I'm just not going to do it anymore.

The number one criterion, for the very first time in my entire life, is no longer how something looks. The criterion is that it doesn't hurt me.

One of the ways we punish ourselves for not being more or better or thinner or stronger is by trying to squeeze ourselves—force ourselves, even—into all kinds of ill-fitting relationships. With other people, with ourselves, with our pants.

In our dysfunction, we spray-lacquer our clothing on, believing it will help us feel better. We only feel worse. Pinched. Squeezed. Restricted. Constricted. As we get well, we see that we no longer need to tolerate things that are hurting us (bad pants, bad boyfriends, bad friends, bad self-talk). We care about ourselves enough to stop confining ourselves. We care about ourselves enough to stop punishing ourselves.

As we get well, we see that we no longer need to tolerate things that are hurting us.

If I'm ever going to be able to make changes in my life, I have to start with practicing radical love toward myself, not contempt. One tangible example is pants. I'm sure you can think of a dozen more.

I cannot deprive, punish, squeeze, or bully myself into feeling good enough. There aren't enough Bad Pants in the world to fill the void. There is only enough Christ.

• • •

Write about one thing you are in an ill-fitting relationship with (your schedule, food, a friendship, your pants, etc).

day 75 DON'T GO BACK TO SLEEP

The breeze at dawn
has secrets to tell you.
Don't go back to sleep.
You must ask
for what you really want.
Don't go back to sleep.
—*Rumi*

I'm always inspired by the part in *On Writing* when Stephen King talks about how he got *Carrie*, his first novel, written. He was living in a double-wide with his wife and his first child, working two—maybe even three—fairly unsavory jobs to make ends meet.

While the rest of his family slept, he would sneak away to this tiny utility room in the double-wide, and he would put a board on his lap and put a typewriter on the board, and he would write. He wrote the entire novel that way. Locked in a closet. With a board on his lap. And a typewriter on the board. While his family slept.

If you read Stephen King's whole story, you would see he had a hundred reasons why that particular time in his life was not the right time to write a novel. Anyone would have agreed. There were so many reasons why he should have waited. But Stephen King had decided what he wanted, and he was going for it. Even if he had to steal the time to do it.

Even without a swanky writing room and a beautiful new MacBook Pro? you ask. Yep. Even without the glitz.

If you are really brave, you're going to decide what you want and you're going to go for it. And to be perfectly honest, it's probably not going to go that well. Not nearly as well as it did for Stephen King.

You probably won't write a bestseller on your first pass, though some of you will. You probably won't make the amount of money you thought you would if you simply followed your dreams. You probably won't gain the fame you had secretly thought you might. This is somewhat devastating because, here you've taken the trouble to decide what you want and you've gone for it. In some ways, it won't deliver. Not in the big, garish ways we had all hoped.

What the going for it *will* deliver, though, is something much more intangible, much more shrouded and mysterious. (Don't you hate that.) It will deliver you back to you, dose by precious dose. Because figuring out what we want, what we really want, wakes us up. So if you are slightly deadened, slightly distanced from your own life, start by asking yourself, *What do I want?*

See what surfaces. Even if *I have no idea* surfaces. That's a fine place to start. Just start somewhere. Whatever you do, don't go back to sleep.

Sometimes you've got to steal time for the things you love, the things that fill you up, your soul's deepest inspiration. The universe isn't going to hand you the time. You have to concoct a way to safely and legally and ethically (in other words, don't steal the time from your boss when you're getting paid to be working) steal a bit of time to fill up. I learned all this from Stephen King.

When we steal time to do the things we love, we find ourselves again and the parts of us that we want to protect and nourish. We find the parts of us that we don't want to let shame or fear or the Soul Bullies silence.

Carve out a corner in this world, steal some time like Stephen King, and get to work. The world is waiting for you. Yes, small little everyday you. Yes, you. Worthy old you. Put the board on your lap. Put the typewriter on the board. And get to work. Steal some time and show up to life. Do it because you want to tell a truer story.

• • •

I would steal time in order to . . .

____

____

____

____

____

day 76 OK, I GET IT

Whoever you are, you are human.
Wherever you are, you live in the world,
which is just waiting for you
to notice the holiness in it.

—Barbara Brown Taylor

I was driving recently and saw a fresh twentysomething walking down the street. She had on enviable boots and her hair was pulled back into a messy-on-purpose chignon and she carried a venti Starbucks and an I've-got-things-together sort of handbag. She wasn't drop-dead gorgeous or anything. She was just clean, freshly washed, clothed and in her right mind, and I was the furthest thing from such ease.

I started crying right there at the red light, watching her float down the street while I felt like nothing more than raw meat.

Shame's siren song whispers in my ear, "You used to be able to handle it all. It's hard to believe you've become such a wreck."

Most of the time, my humanity makes me feel so fleshy and exposed, which I don't particularly appreciate. As a human, I am not immune to grief, to struggle, to dark nights, to poor hygiene. I've had to accept all this. And yet it's my humanity—my soft center—that makes me stop and take notice of moments like this:

I was in the car—again—creeping slowly down the stretch of road in Coronado that parallels the beach. That day, I saw a miracle.

A big daddy was carrying his little girl. She was sandy and sun-smooched and her head bobbed up and down on his shoulder as he walked. Her limp arms were dangled over his shoulders as she slept.

"I get it," I said out loud in the car. "OK, I get it."

Some days we will feel pulverized. Absolutely meat-cleavered. Triggered in a thousand different ways. Our fretting about how we might do better or be more or how we could have avoided the struggle if we would have been a prettier or more talented person will only ever make things feel so much worse. We will zing and ping and ding around in a stratosphere that has nothing to do with what actually matters. We will exhaust ourselves to the point of paralysis.

The father-daughter moment broke into my zinging. Those two were about the deeper anchors of life: love, care, nurture, trust, grace.

The two of them were just walking down the street toward their car after a full day by the sea. Very simple and yet very profound. They are what is true. What remains. What matters. Holding and being held. Resting. Connecting. Loving and being loved. Beauty and the broad grace.

• • •

Today, this is what actually matters:

day 77 OFFERING OURSELVES PERMISSION TO DO THINGS DIFFERENTLY

> *May the words of my mouth*
> *and the meditation of my heart*
> *be acceptable to you,*
> *LORD, my rock and my Redeemer.*
> —*Psalm 19:14 CSB*

The word *permission* is, in its origin, a "noun of action" in Latin. Permission can seem passive, an allowance or acquiescence. In reality, it's a conscious decision.

Offering permission is an act of personal responsibility. When life feels like it's happening to us, offering ourselves permission to do things differently is a way to live intentionally. We are paying homage to the fact that we always have options. We have, always available to us, a noun of action.

For the longest time, the reality that I had options had completely slipped my mind.

We can offer ourselves permission to rest, to get help, to stop, to breathe. We can offer ourselves permission to pursue a passion, to dream, to forgive, to get on the treadmill.

We don't have to wait. We can effect change.

Stress, chaos, urgency, and panic don't have to control our lives. We actually have a say. We can allow ourselves the dignity of responding to our circumstances, even changing our circumstances, instead of just resigning to them.

Some of us are making the people around us miserable because we won't wake up and take personal responsibility for ourselves, our decisions, and our pain. We're defensive when we should be proactive. We're woeful when we could be whole. I don't know about you, but I want to be brave enough to get unstuck, to not hold my loved ones hostage by my inability to take personal responsibility for my wellness.

Growth and healing start by giving ourselves the permission to pursue them. If we aren't willing to show up and participate, then chances are, our souls will be lost on some level. And chances are, it will affect the people who want to share life with us.

• • •

I am offering myself permission to . . .

____

____

____

day 78 MAKING COMMITMENTS TO OURSELVES

The most useful piece of learning for the uses of life is to unlearn what is untrue.

—Antisthenes

One of the things that gets all tangled up in making a commitment to ourselves and following through is our fear.

What if it doesn't turn out perfectly?

What if I fail?

What if no one notices?

What if it's hard?

What if I don't have any support?

What if people don't get it?

What if ______ could do it better?

What if I work so, so, so hard and it doesn't end up mattering anyway?

What if I'm disappointed?

What if I end up with regrets?
What if . . . ?

I rehearse these what-ifs all the time.

What if I work for years and it never amounts to anything?
What if no one gets it?
What if I'm running out of time?
What if she beats me to it?
What if I'm just an amateur?
What if it's too hard?

These are the days when I'm stuck in my own closed loop, believing (erroneously) that life is only all about the product, when I have come to realize that life is actually so much more about the process.

Entering into the process is nearly always a mess. We will never be able to do things perfectly and glamorously all the time. Tragic, I know. What we're talking about here is walking into the mess and trusting that the process itself has great gifts to offer if we will get up off the couch and participate.

Life is going to hand us Hard over and over again. Here's what you and I can do:

You make a pact with yourself, something manageable. And you keep that pact. You firmly treat yourself with gentleness. That's the key. You love yourself too much to let yourself fade away.

You do this because you care about being alive and awake in the world, about being conscious, about inhabiting your own life. You do this because you want to make some kind of small or large contribution, because you want to be whole.

You do this as a way to honor your true self. Not out of anxious striving but out of a deeper calling, you peck away. A tiny bit at a time. For the long haul. You are unwilling to live with an untold story. You are unwilling to silence your one and only voice.

Over time, you will look back at the body of work you've created, or the personal growth you've experienced, or the memories you've made with your children, or the connection you feel with your partner, or the incremental progress you've made professionally, and you'll see that these small commitments and your follow-through have actually added up.

Over time . . . you'll see that these small commitments and your follow-through have actually added up.

Just shows you what you can do when you lean into the Hard, when you get in touch with that warrior within. We learn to believe in ourselves again when we face challenges with courage. We will not conquer everything in our path. We may not have perfect abs while going into battle, but we can still fight. We can still push up against life a bit. We can still show up. We can still arise and put on our war paint!

Hey, life, I'm here. I'm not going to let you beat me. I'm not going to drift out to sea. Period. Even if the only easy day was yesterday. Bring. It. On.

And if it all goes sideways (because it will, at some point), I will take a nap or a hot shower and then I will come for you again. I will begin again. I will put on the war paint AGAIN. Hear me roar.

I'm not sure what you're working on today. Perhaps you're working on a creative project, realizing a dream, getting/staying sober, or surviving a divorce. Maybe you're working on grief today because grief is like a job sometimes. Maybe you're working on a new business venture, homeschool curriculum, a big decision, a friendship, a vegetable garden, or getting your baby to sleep through the night. Maybe you've just moved or maybe you're barely moving.

Whatever you want to get accomplished today, here's to making a commitment to yourself, keeping that commitment, celebrating the doing of it, and pushing up against fear.

• • •

What is a fear that is getting in the way of something important you are (or want to be) working on?

___

___

___

day 79 POSTURE OF PLENTY

For God *is sheer beauty,*
all-generous in love,
loyal always and ever.
—Psalm 100:5

Plenty means "fullness," an invitation to see our circumstances as more than just one-dimensional. Whether we're stuck on the floor with small children, stuck in a job we don't love, stuck in a bed from illness, we can still find fullness—though it might not be evident at first glance.

We are not without.

There is plenty of love.

Plenty of hope.

Plenty of friendship.

Plenty of creativity.

Plenty of laughter.

Plenty of time.

Plenty of beauty.

Even one friend is plenty, if we learn to do life together.

Life offers us so much more than enough. We have, at our fingertips, plenty. The most revolutionary thing we can do is choose to see the fullness instead of the lack, no matter where life has us.

We look for plenty as a reminder of his kingdom come.

• • •

God, Thank you for giving me plenty of . . .

____

____

____

____

____

day 80 THE WANDERING ISN'T FUTILE

The ragamuffin who sees his life as a voyage of discovery and runs the risk of failure has a better feel for faithfulness than the timid man who hides behind the law and never finds out who he is at all.

—Brennan Manning

When you start over, you have to start over. Those are the rules.

In your new environment, there's so much to take in, so many new things to adjust to. With all the adjusting and learning and beginning again, life can feel like perpetual wandering.

Not arriving can be so painful. Waiting can be so painful. That seeming lack of progress. The feeling that we're not getting anywhere. But it's in the wandering that we pick up new truths, stumble across new paths, acquire unforeseen knowledge, link up with companions and guides.

How might our anxiety levels and our toxic thinking change if we were to see ourselves as experiencers and not require ourselves to be experts? How might we be inspired to risk courageously, love generously, live expectantly if we could accept the journey?

Sometimes it's OK to just not know, to not know the end from the beginning, to not understand how we're going to get there from here.

Being a companion to ourselves means we don't have to fix it or figure it out. Instead, we can flex. Take the next step. More will be revealed. We can pray for God to help us tolerate the waiting and the seeming lack of control, to help us focus on what we can control, which is how we treat ourselves in the middle of the uncertainty.

No matter where you are today, I believe the work is within you. I believe in your capacity to step into that work and live. We must all meet on the common road of needing-God-in-our-humanity. If we could see the answer from here, we wouldn't need courage. We wouldn't need God. We wouldn't need each other. We wouldn't need faith.

Faith says, I will let myself be led by a power that is higher than I am, by someone who can see what I can't see from here.

Sometimes all we've been given is a match when what we were hoping for and waiting for was high beams. But if we'll commit to what's right in front of us, we can make the long journey with just a little light at a time.

• • •

God, I am so weary of the wandering. Please give me what I need for this journey. I am asking specifically for…

___

___

___

day 81 THIS IS OUR STORY

I have woven a parachute out of everything broken.

—William Stafford

My pastor once told a story I have never forgotten. It's the story of a little girl who had been born with a cleft palate. When her classmates asked her what happened to her face, she would tell them she fell down and cut it on glass because it seemed so much more tolerable to have had an accident than to have been born "this way."

Her second-grade teacher, Miss Leonard, was everyone's favorite teacher. Each year, when it was time for the kids to have their hearing tested, Miss Leonard would stand on one side of the door and whisper something to the child who was standing with their ear to the other side of the door. The children would then repeat what Miss Leonard said to them: "You have new shoes." Or "Your shirt is green." When it was the little girl with the cleft palate's turn for her whisper test, she put her ear to the door and she heard Miss Leonard whisper to her, "I wish you were my little girl."

This is our story. We come to the door with our maladies and brokenness only to be received with revolutionary love. We come to the door with our jumbled-up fear and worry and our ferocious intensity, and we are met with grace. We come to the door, and we realize Christ was there knocking, all along.

Hear Christ's words spoken over you today: "I am so glad you are mine. Just as you are. Just as I created you to be. I am so, so grateful you are mine." Make your decisions, love your people, move into your day from this place, knowing he is always greeting you with wide-open arms.

• • •

God, thank you that I am yours and you are mine.
Please remind me of who you say I am.

____

____

____

____

____

day 82 MY LOVABILITY IS NOT CONTINGENT

Self-acceptance is my refusal to be in an adversarial relationship with myself.
—Nathanial Branden

It's easy to feel loved when you're riding high, performing well, on top of your game. It's more difficult to access those feelings of worthiness and unconditional acceptance when things have gone awry and your humanity is poking out of every seam.

Last week the preschool was trying to get in touch with me and I missed their call(s) because the ringer on my phone was turned off. The whole situation resolved, thanks to the rescue efforts of Tina, who ended up having to go to the preschool and take my child home with her until I could be reached. I felt embarrassed and low. I'd let go of it, so I thought, until it was time to show my face at the preschool again this morning and my mind immediately started rehearsing all the reasons why I was unfit for duty.

I was reminded of the two party invitations that slipped through the cracks and the emails I'm behind on. I could feel the accusations closing in, and then I spilled my coffee everywhere . . . because when the bullies are coming for you, you feel rattled and shaky.

As I was paper-toweling coffee from the counter to the trash can, I remembered one of the all-time most helpful concepts in the universe: sometimes we just need to begin again. Because we really, truly don't arrive. We just return to the truth. I had to remember to treat myself with care and compassion. I had to remember to breathe. I had to remember to reach out and ask God to remind me that my lovability is not contingent on how well I execute the logistics of life.

Because we really, truly don't arrive. We just return to the truth.

And God reminded me of something important, essential even: I am never more loved than in the moment of my failings, my faltering, my humanity. I'm never more loved than the moment when it all falls apart. I turn on myself when things crash—especially if the crash happens on my watch—but God doesn't. He doesn't turn on me—ever. In fact, the total opposite, he wants to love me through my Come Apart if I'll let him.

(Ugghhh, it's practically impossible to tolerate that kind of persistent grace.)

Through God, we've been offered a love that is based solely on someone loving us, totally divested of anything we bring to the table. We're loved, even when we're average, unorganized, plagued, tired, ineffective, worried, and/or totally unspectacular. It's radical, isn't it? Radical, I think, because so many of us have a warped experience of love.

One of the most courageous things we can do is stare down this love God is offering us and ask ourselves if we really, truly believe it's real. Do you believe you are loved like that? In your worst moments, in your deepest doubts, in your greatest failures, when the preschool can't get ahold of you . . . are you loved?

Every single day, we each must get up and answer that question for ourselves. Because the way we answer that question really does affect everything.

• • •

My lovability is not contingent on . . .

day 83 NOT DYING ISN'T THE SAME THING AS LIVING

What if you wake up some day, and you're 65 . . . and you were just so strung out on perfectionism and people-pleasing that you forgot to have a big juicy creative life?

—Anne Lamott

I am so often waiting for all the Hard to dissipate before I believe I can really live. But perhaps the solution isn't the absence of the Hard, it's what we do when we're in the midst of it. Will we succumb to colorless, motionless, woefulness, martyrdom?

Or will we persevere, look for the hope?

Sometimes, for a season, all we can expect from ourselves is to sit on the floor and breathe. And that's plenty. But then, after a week or a month or a year or three, after we have caught our breath, we must do the work of remembering that our issues are not the same thing as our identity. We must emerge.

Walking into living color is vulnerable. So very vulnerable. It's like coming out from a dark room and you have to squint to tolerate the light. But at some point we have to consider the truth Eep Crood already told us, in the movie *The Croods*, when she said, "Dad, not dying isn't the same thing as living."

We let our eyes open again. We let our hearts and souls wake up instead of believing that life and faith and healing and recovery are one big trick.

We do the brazen work of going after the "you" and the "me" that's been hiding, buried, muted, lost, abandoned. We invest in our own healing. We do it as a debt of honor to ourselves and as our most profound worship to God, our Creator. We will not live in the dark, even if that means we have to walk around squinting for a time. We will let ourselves be seen. We will let ourselves be free. We will emerge.

There is no perfect time to be courageous. Our emergence doesn't happen when we are at our most brave. It often happens when we are at our most bruised. We choose to lean into the tears and the fears and the dreams and the wild and we decide we will not hide.

• • •

God, show me the ways in which I am settling for not-dying instead of real-living.

day 84 20 MINUTES OF SOUL TIME

If she got really quiet and listened,
new parts of her wanted to speak.
—Susan Ariel

I can fall back on being a "try-er" by nature. Someone who muscles through. Once I've tried and tried and tried, then I find I'm so tired. Funny how *tried* and *tired* are practically the same word if you look at them side by side.

By "try" here, I mean the frantic strive, hustle, press. I'm not saying some endeavors in life aren't difficult, challenging, requiring work. But work is different from that endless try.

Work has a destination.
Try is a treadmill.

When all our effort runs out, when all our chasing is exhausted, when all our solving proves futile, when all our analysis is in vain . . . then, and only then, do we happen upon a space where we are totally quiet before God. I wonder if this is where he wanted us all along. Perhaps all God wants is to get us still enough so he can pat our arm gently and say, *Shh, it's OK. Shh. I'm here.* This is grace, and it trumps our try every single day of the week.

Few things have taught me about grace—and it's unforced-ness—like the practice of twenty minutes of soul time. Making space to get really quiet and listen is holy work. We happen upon God personally and we are gifted with a sustaining encounter. I believe encounters reveal what our efforts never could.

I take my legal pad out to the courtyard at the front of our house, and I smell the jasmine overgrowing the gate down below the courtyard, feel the wind, and hear the music created by the movement in the palm fronds. I turn my face toward the sun, the warmth and light.

Just this—walking outside and breathing in the world, if we will make time to do it—is intoxicating. Taking time to receive the aliveness of the world and be energized by its essence.

I take a couple of deep breaths as a means of finding my way back to my body. I can so easily be floating outside my own existence, and this practice is an opportunity to find my way back to myself. So I breathe and try to settle down into my seat, and I listen to whatever is stirring up in my soul.

What am I afraid of? What anxieties am I carrying? What am I worried about? Where does my body hurt? What longings are lurking? What angst is making me crazy? What tension am I experiencing? Any feelings that have energy behind them get recorded. Again, I'm not trying to make sense of anything. I'm simply showing up, keeping my pen moving, trying to take notes for my soul.

After about ten to fifteen minutes of soul-recording, I write, *God, what do you want to say to me about all this?*

This step is so important because it formally invites God into my tangles. Of course he's already there, already waiting for me, but I need to be reminded of that fact, reminded that he wants to offer wisdom, comfort, love, truth. So I ask him what he wants to tell me, and then I listen and write, listen and write. I do all this until my phone timer chimes.

Here's the linchpin: I ask God to help me let go and embrace the flow of what surfaces, instead of judging, analyzing, evaluating the contents of my soul and his responses. For those twenty minutes, I'm not allowed to be a soul skeptic. I'm not allowed to reach for holds. I am to submit to the tide.

• • •

God, tell me what you want me to know today.

____

____

____

____

____

day 85 DON'T FIGHT THE RIVER

He who has ears to hear, let him hear.

—Matthew 11:15 ESV

This summer I took my kids up to Tahoe to visit family. One morning we ventured out to the Yuba River with our clunky water shoes and coolers and giant tubes. The Clampetts go to Tahoe. The water was so clear you could see down to the river floor, and despite the drought in California, the water ran just fast enough that we could catch a ride.

We took turns escorting the littlest cousins down the river while the big kids drank grape soda on the shore. After a couple of attempts, we were all learning how to best maneuver our tubes between rocks, other tubers, the minor-league rapids. My son Luke said it best after his first run: "Well, there's one thing I've learned already: Don't fight the river."

Yes. This is the image we are to take with us into our twenty minutes of soul time. We are to trust the flow.

Here's how you do it:

Order a couple things on Amazon—a pack of brand-new legal pads or a journal that seems compelling. Find a pen that speaks to you and a place in your world that nurtures you. Light a candle you love or make a fire in the fireplace. Get your coffee the way you like it or pour your sparkling water into a pretty glass.

Set a timer and write and listen, write and listen.

And then a few days later, do it again. That's it.

As an extrovert with a busy brain, I find it almost embarrassingly obvious that I would need to sit down and be still. So obvious, in fact, that I don't do it. And then my brain gets busier and my body gets buzzier, and the next thing you know I've dis-integrated, and I'm a head walking around with lots of ideas and lots of plans and lots of solutions . . . and no soul.

As we listen to ourselves, we create space for God. And as we encounter God, we find ourselves.

No one benefits from this version of me. Sure, my people will love me even when I'm in this state, but I am not the me I was created to be. And therefore, I suffer in this equation too, because I am completely disconnected from the Source. As we listen to ourselves, we create space for God. And as we encounter God, we find ourselves.

I think every one of us is longing for an encounter with God. For something true that intersects with our real lives and our real needs. We long to not just study about him, but to meet with him. And, even more, to meet with him in a way that has bearing on what is actually going on in our own lives. To hear him speaking over us. To feel him reaching toward us.

Your soul is where all of you and all of God dwells. You don't analyze, think, or study your way there. You push the urgent back and you sit and you listen. You come to a point where you realize the rest of your life isn't going to work if this twenty minutes doesn't happen regularly. It's a recalibration. It's a reintegration. In those twenty minutes, allow yourself to be met with grace. Again, this isn't about you working your way to God. This is about you sitting down long enough for God to get to you.

Desires will surface. Memories will walk right toward you. You might see yourself as a child. You might remember a dream you hadn't thought about in years. You might think of something you love. Your soul time may not produce immediate answers—then again, it might. It's not a time to analyze or fix. It's a time of flow, like Lukey on the Yuba.

This is how we learn to live from love instead of living for looks. We slow down long enough to listen and receive the love that is ours for the taking. We let it seep into the deepest parts of our being. In the past, we were moving so fast, talking such a streak, that the goodness would just run off. Now we allow our soul to be soaked—down to the root—and then we get up from the chair and we go about our day from that soul-soaked place.

We allow God to chip away at the plaster we've packed around our fleshy, vulnerable soul. It's about returning to what he's already given us. Returning instead of relentlessly forging ahead. So the challenge for all of us will be creating enough space to practice what we know, and then simply believing God at his Word: that as we come to him, we trade our try for his rest.

Take a deep breath and get quiet. Then quieter still. What is God speaking into that true place inside you?

(Remember, don't fight the river.)

• • •

Set your phone timer for five minutes. Listen and write down what you hear. Practice not editing or judging what surfaces.

day 86 EXPAND INSTEAD OF EDIT

Life shrinks or expands in proportion to one's courage.

—Anais Nin

A long time ago I was talking to a middle-aged woman who was bookish and wore sensible shoes and she told me she danced on the beach as her way of experiencing God.

When she told me this, I was struck dumb. I stood there looking at her with my mouth open, thinking, *I'm sorry, what did you say?* Not only was I shocked by her audacity, I was also very aware of a big feeling welling up in me.

I was so envious of her freedom. To be Plain Jane and to dance and dance and dance. Right there on the beach.

To me, dancing is the embodiment of freedom. I'm a self-conscious dancer. I don't even really wish I were a better dancer. I just wish I were a freer dancer. And the bookish woman, dancing her prayers to God, was *free*.

Recently I was at the beach, and I got up off my blanket and stepped into the ocean, which was ice cold and immediately refreshing. I looked down, the water so shallow and clear that you could see gold in the sand I was standing on. Like someone had dumped glitter everywhere.

I looked it up later. It's mica. Tiny flecks of heaven.

I let the water splash up my leggings. Farther than I had intended, but it was so hot outside, and it felt good. The coldness felt like it was literally draining the inflammation from my feet, which looked like sausages under the water.

I thought about Plain Jane. I thought about all the ways I'm tempted to be rigid and ruled. And the little voice inside my soul said, "Expand. Expand instead of edit. Expand, Leeana."

(Which, of course, is gold.)

. . .

Is there an invitation to expand where you have only previously edited yourself?

____

____

____

____

____

____

day 87 KEEP CASTING YOUR NETS

It was my letting go that gave me a better hold.

—*Chris Matakas*

I have the words "keep casting your nets" written on a kraft envelope and taped to the wall above my desk.

This simple sentence, from a story in the book of John, is offering me some calibration these days. It's a reminder that my response, much more than my results, is what creates meaning in my life. To the point that sometimes I feel like God is saying to me, *Frankly, Leeana, the results are none of your business.*

According to the account in Scripture, the disciples were out on the Sea of Galilee fishing. They had spent the entire night casting their nets but caught nothing. Not. One. Thing. It's dawn. They're exhausted. Their labors seem futile. And someone calls to them from the shore. It's Jesus, though they don't know that immediately. He says, "Cast your nets again on the right side of the boat."

They do, and their nets are so full they can't haul in the catch.

keep = continue showing up bravely

casting = offering

your = no one else's

nets = what God has put in your hands

I cast laundry into the washing machine and then into the dryer. I cast dishes into warm, soapy water. I cast tubes of yogurt into lunch bags and meals into the oven. I cast words into the world. I cast love out to my children, my family, my friends. Some days, this feels mostly effortless, like I'm smack-dab in the center of what I was made to do and be. And then there are the other days. When I'm filled with self-doubt because nothing seems to be working.

And God says, *Keep doing the work I have given you today. Continue the work of feeding, nurturing, creating, ideating, hoping, holding, wondering, believing, listening. Keep doing the sacred work. Do not grow weary in doing good because at the right time, the fullness will materialize (Gal. 6:9).*

Trusting our try over the mystery of God's miracles is not freedom; it's fear. Paralysis and cynicism are ways we distrust him and doubt ourselves. He's asking us to show up, come out from behind our fear of failure or fear of purposelessness. We have the choice whether or not we will do the vulnerable work of showing up.

Participation, not perfection, is what's so brazen.

Every day, God asks me to cast the nets of mothering, mending, and making. Some days I'm sure I don't have what it takes to offer what God is asking me to offer. These words taped to my wall serve as a reminder to keep showing up even on the days when I'm plagued with self-doubt, even on the days when I'm a stammering Moses. Even on those days, which are most days, when I am to keep giving my offering.

What's interesting is that the etymology of the word *offering* implies a sacrificial element. So it follows that our offering is not something we come by easily. It's something we fight for. It's something that costs us. I will not offer that which costs me nothing (2 Sam. 24:24).

An offering is something we give away. It's something we let go of. It's something we set down. You can't really offer something and keep your hands on it. You're giving this love, this creation, this artistry, this contribution, this dream . . . away.

. . .

What are you holding on to that you need to give away?

day 88 WHAT IN YOUR LIFE IS IN NEED OF A RESURRECTION?

Jesus himself came up and walked along with them;
but they were kept from recognizing him.

—*Luke 24:15–16 NIV*

Right before Easter, I got the news that my very first book had gone out of print. And it stung. It is incredibly difficult to watch something important die, whether that's a relationship, a person, a desire, a dream. You never get used to it. I don't think death ever becomes less abrupt.

But the invitation I kept hearing over and over was to identify an area of my life that needed a resurrection and then *believe* that a resurrection could be possible. In other words, hope. Not the noun *hope*, the verb *hope*. To hope. Actively.

The ability to hope comes from the idea that what we believe is the end may only be the beginning. Which, of course, is the story of Jesus. For Easter, my pastor spoke on the passage in Luke 24 when Cleopas and his companion are walking on the road to Emmaus and the resurrected Jesus joins them, but they don't know it's him.

The story reads, "Jesus himself came up and walked along with them; but they were kept from recognizing him."

I can think of a few really big things in my life that could use an injection of breath and heartbeat and spirit and vitality. And there's a certain dangerousness to hoping because it puts us out there on a limb of desire that may not produce.

But I don't think the cynics win. I don't think hopelessness wins. And the story from the road to Emmaus makes me wonder if it's at all possible that, in fact, Jesus himself is walking in my midst and maybe I'm just not yet recognizing him.

For me, one of the ways Jesus himself is walking with me right now is through a question Langston Hughes raises in his poem "Harlem": What happens when our hopes and dreams go unfulfilled? Do they die or do they explode?

What happened to Jesus and his followers and their dreams of a new way of living and loving and believing? What happened at the cross? Did it all dry up? Or did it explode?

I'm holding on to the Easter story today as a reminder that sometimes what we believe is an ending may very well be the beginning. And with Jesus, new is always near.

Death stings.
Hope explodes.

• • •

What in your life is in need of a resurrection?

day 89 I LOVE EVERY VERSION OF YOU

Just in case you ever foolishly forget,
I am never not thinking about you.
—Virginia Woolf

I absolutely love David Benner's idea that "God's deepest desire for us is to replace our fig leaves with garments of durability and beauty."

I think this is one of the deepest longings of our heart: that we could shed our false protections and believe the God-in-us is enough. Our false attachments, our clinging to cover, help us forget about our nakedness. God doesn't want us to cover our own nakedness. He wants us to turn to him in our vulnerability and allow him to robe us, clothe us in his love.

My friend Elaine told me recently, "I love every version of you."

Have you ever had someone look you in the eye and tell you that? The night before I had been ranting about something, started ugly crying, and the next day I started grabbing for the fig leaves. I felt embarrassed that I had let her see me like that, in a state that felt out of control, snotty. She offered me something I couldn't offer myself: no condemnation. Unconditional love. She reminded me that my garments are made of durability and beauty, and I do not need to shroud myself in shame.

God does the very same thing for us. He reaches toward us and says, *I love every version of you, you gorgeous thing.*

We can put those words on like the gown they are, and whisper, "Sorry, shame. I am ready to live wildly loved."

• • •

God, I believe you love every version of me, even . . .

day 90 THE POWER OF SELF-POSSESSION

The mind I love must have wild places.
—Katherine Mansfield

I'd like to settle into my own skin a bit more than the adolescent me ever did. She leaned heavy on applause, and she got it, but I'm ready for something more than acceptance at this stage of my life. I'm longing to be self-possessed.

When you think of a person who is self-possessed, think about someone who knows what she believes, knows her own opinions, knows her own tastes, and isn't trying to morph or chameleon into what the next person walking toward her needs her to be. She has a sense of herself and she lives true to that sense, honoring it.

She has a strength of intuition, and she's loyal to her Created Center. She can practice her "no" with confidence because she's in tune with her own needs, her family's needs, her soul's needs, and she isn't going to allow the requests of others to bulldoze her priorities and her capacity.

And if someone manages to get close to her and then they abuse that closeness, she is able to rescue herself. She's able to stand up for her own existence and politely excuse herself from the relationship. If the other person thinks she's a heartless witch for doing so, that's fine. Because the self-possessed woman knows, surely, that she is not a heartless witch. She is, in fact, a soul warrior.

She has spent extended periods of time in the presence of God, listening to the deep-waters voice of God that teaches her to honor her family, honor her craft, honor her desires, honor what has been put in her hands. She knows she is God-possessed, and so she is able to be confidently self-possessed.

Her limits and her boundaries aren't just a "no" to intruders. They are about protecting her "deeper yes," the yes she has fought to discover in the presence of God. Her creative space. Her quiet mornings. Her kids' bedtime. Her night out with her husband. Her sanity. Her God-image. The self-possessed woman is learning that a well-tended life requires these touchstones, and she will be angry if she allows other people's agendas for her to rob her of her life rhythm.

Sometimes I find myself angry with the offending party. Don't they know they're crossing my boundaries? Don't they know that's too much to ask? Don't they know that's not going to work for me? All my energy is directed at the other person when I'm actually really frustrated with me. When I refuse to rescue myself from the boundary bulldozers, I'm choosing to keep everyone happy with me instead of living my own truth. This is me silencing my own voice, refusing to be the soul warrior I want to be. This is me being others-possessed, not self-possessed, for a self-possessed person takes responsibility for herself and her life.

I'm just now learning it's OK to say . . .

I don't know.

I don't like that.

I don't want that.

I can't do that.

I need help.

I need to think about it.

I'm not sure.

I don't think that will work for me.

I need to go now.

No, thank you.

No, you can't.

In other words, I'm just now learning how to articulate—out loud—inconvenient truths. Not to be rigid or jerky just for the sake of getting in people's faces—belligerence is every bit as adolescent as people-pleasing—but to protect those things that matter most to me.

I'll tell you some of the biggest ways we stay in hiding: Worry far more about being liked than being known. Worry far more about wooing others than honoring ourselves. Worry far more about keeping the peace than finding our voice. Worry far more about control than figuring out who we are.

So where do we start?

We start by talking to God about the "deeper yes" of our lives, asking him to help us discover or rediscover those pursuits and people worth protecting our time and energy for. And then we tell the truth, which is so much harder than I imagined. But you know what's even harder than telling the truth? Looking back and realizing you never quite had the time to really live.

Is someone or something in your life bulldozing your boundaries? What is keeping you from protecting, possessing, your boundary?

day 91 WHAT GOD HAS DONE

In the future, when your children ask you, "What do these stones mean?" tell them that the flow of the Jordan was cut off before the ark of the covenant of the Lord. *When it crossed the Jordan, the waters of the Jordan were cut off. These stones are to be a memorial to the people of Israel forever.*

—Joshua 4:6–7 NIV

In 2004, I was living in the Middle East with my brand-new husband, and God whispered in my ear—definitively—that I was to be a writer. Additionally, he opened a very big door for me to begin my public writing journey.

When something this significant happens, I am a firm believer in never forgetting. To that end, I decided to commemorate the entire journey with a tattoo.

Nothing about getting the tattoo hurt physically. I think I was in such a state of borderline panic about it that I was numb to the pain. My memory is only of the anxiety I felt around getting it done.

The tattoo commemorates this journey: God's whisper in my ear all those years ago—in our flat overlooking the Persian Gulf—that sent my heart pounding and my fingers flying on the keyboard and started me down a path that I am still very much in awe of today.

The tattoo commemorates a Come Apart season for me and the tenderness and struggle and overwhelmed-ness that birthed me fighting for myself in new ways. And this tattoo commemorates me, showing up with my big voice, even though I get scared. Even though.

The biggest obstacle for me with this tattoo was not the fear of the pain. It definitely wasn't "comfortable," but I have been through much worse pain, for sure. Essentially, everything related to childbirth.

My biggest obstacle to getting this tattoo was what people would think.

We all have a Soul Bully that is constantly telling us how we should be doing things. This voice never takes into consideration what's actually happening in our lives, the reality of our particular circumstances. It stands far off, making blanket judgments about what it means to be "good" and what it means to be "bad." This is every bit as unhelpful as it sounds.

I am asking God to help me heal from this disease of needing to know that everyone approves of everything I'm doing and saying. Of not wanting to disappoint anyone. Of not wanting to displease in any way. So, maybe as much as anything, this tattoo commemorates my brave step toward letting go of what others may or may not be thinking and welcoming my own desires. This is actually deep, incisive work for me. Goes to the core. The struggle between wanting to own my voice and yet not wanting to make any waves with it. This is the work I will continue to do, and I hope that every time I look down at my arm, I will be inspired anew to be brazen.

So many of us are dying to connect with that Soul Voice inside us, struggling to set him or her free, desperate to celebrate—shamelessly—our unique expressions of self. We are longing for a touch from God's transcendent hand that shifts everything, absolutely everything. And we need someone to give us the permission to be true to the work of God in our lives, letting go of how others believe we might need to be doing it.

Of course I don't think you need to get a tattoo to be your true self or to celebrate God's work in your life. But for me, this was a huge step in owning my own story, my own voice, and my own creativity.

The tattoo is designed to look like henna, inspired by the Middle East. I chose aqua ink. And I chose to put it on my right arm because that is my writing hand.

On those occasions when we begin to find our Soul Voice, begin to offer it out into the world, we must commemorate our clarity and our courage. We must memorialize the transformative work of God in our lives. We can do that any ol' way that feels meaningful to us personally—stacking our very own stones of remembrance.

In a journal. Up our arm. With a paintbrush. Over coffee. On a prayer. In a message in a bottle.

So that we never forget what God has done.

• • •

What's something God has done in your life that you'd like to memorialize? How can you create a visual reminder (a memorial that you will see) to help you remember?

____

____

____

day 92 PERFECT FREEDOM

It is for freedom that Christ has set us free.
—Galatians 5:1 NIV

A few years ago, we needed to make a decision about where to send the twins to elementary school. Our neighborhood public school had a fabulous reputation, was one mile from our house, and was rated a 10 out of 10 in the California public schools. But I was afraid.

Afraid of the unknown, mainly. I grew up very near the same neighborhood, but I did not go to that school, so I didn't have a lot of context for it. Additionally, many of my friends were putting their kids in other schools, so I was worried about what that would look like for us and for our kids socially.

In his book *Integrity*, Dr. Henry Cloud introduced a new-to-me definition of the word *integrity*: "the courage to meet the demands of reality."[1]

I have held on to that idea since first reading it.

Not run. Not hide. Not snivel. Not panic. Not freeze. Not escape. But instead, meet. Show up and be present and meet today, with whatever it holds. Integrate instead of disintegrate.

Life is full of big decisions, moments that create a trajectory in a certain direction. Rarely are those decisions and that momentum and that trajectory undoable, but still, we want to make the "right" decision the first time.

We want to feel at peace with where we've landed and we don't want to have to go through the pain of undoing something that we've done. Right?

So with all this being true, it's easy to get stuck. I decided to borrow some words from Scripture and turned the whole mess over to God: *I need wisdom, God, so I'm asking for some (James 1:5).*

And here is the only thing I kept hearing from him: *Leeana, do not make a decision based on fear. Don't let fear be the impetus. Don't let fear be your guiding principle. Instead, what decision would you make, Leeana, if you felt perfect freedom?*

I began to think about what I would do if I felt perfect freedom. I learned a lot about whom I was trying to please, my own stories I was projecting onto my kids, my assumptions and generalizations, my places of pride. This entire kindergarten decision was also uprooting the reality that I wasn't sure I could trust my own intuition, which is a disorienting discovery.

Sometimes having the courage to meet the demands of reality means we move forward, even imperfectly, and fight against the temptation to stay stuck.

Sometimes having the courage to meet the demands of reality means we move forward, even imperfectly, and fight against the temptation to stay stuck. We fight against the wallowing. We fight against the paralysis. We decide to believe we are, in fact, reliable observers in this world. Somehow.

Someway.

We get up and brush our teeth. We go for a walk. We take a vitamin. We read one psalm. Or even just one line of one psalm. We say a simple prayer, like, "God, I need you." We get moving in one way or another. I think this is profound.

We decide that we will have the courage to meet the demands of reality. This is the kind of woman I want to be. One who is not guided by fear. One who does not react to life to appease my fear, but one who acknowledges the fear—welcomes it, even—and then moves forward in spite of being afraid.

When I asked myself what I'd do if I wasn't afraid, the decision came to me with ease. Put the kids in the school right in our neighborhood. We did. And I never had a single regret.

• • •

What would you do if you felt perfect freedom?

day 93 YOU ARE THAT GIRL

you will be lost and unlost. over and over again. relax love.
you were meant to be this glorious. epic. story.
—nayyirah waheed

Recently I attended an art workshop with my friend Elaine. During part of the workshop we were invited to roam around the room and pick up objects to include in the art piece we were creating. Objects that spoke to us. Objects we were intuitively drawn to. Objects that told our story even if we didn't know the story yet.

Elaine saw a large peacock feather she immediately loved. She circled it a few times, even reached for it. But she didn't pick it up.

Four of us were sharing a long rectangular table, and when we all returned to the table with our supplies to begin working on our art piece, we were inspecting each other's found objects. As our hands moved, our mouths began to move, and Elaine confessed there was a gorgeous peacock feather she really wanted, but she didn't grab it.

"Why?" we all asked.

"I guess because I didn't think I deserved it," she said before she had time to edit her answer.

We all stopped what we were doing and looked up at her.

And before any of us said anything to her, Elaine said, "I should go get the feather, huh?"

"Yep," we all said in unison.

And she did. It was gorgeous and bigger than many of the other objects on the table.

When I saw it, I could see why it felt presumptuous to her to take it and use it. Like perhaps it was a waste. Or, as she said, it was too special and too lovely to be deserved. I could see why she was immediately and intuitively drawn to it, and I could also see why she couldn't take it right away. It represented the "she" she hopes to be, but couldn't quite believe she already is.

What this tells me is that likely, somewhere inside even the most centered of us all is a place where we are uncertain, adolescent, not quite sure what the rules are and how they apply to us. We perceive someone else to be holding the whistle and, if we move toward something we are assuredly not supposed to have, the whistle will be blown.

But here's what I want you to know . . .

You are that girl. Even if you don't think you are. Even if your mother has spent your lifetime convincing you that you aren't. Even if you had teachers or coaches or mentors or friends or partners or church leaders or colleagues who spent time and energy trying to convince you that you would never, in the history of ever, be worthy.

And I'm so sorry. I'm sorry they knocked you down. I'm sorry they assumed it was OK to come after you and damage you in those ways. I'm sorry they did violence to your soul. I'm sorry they never really saw you.

I hope you have a giant screaming circle of Warrior Sisters in your actual, real life. People who are just nuts about you and tell you all the time that you are gold. But if by chance you don't, I will stop right here and tell you what I know to be true: You are that girl.

At some point in life—maybe even today—you're going to metaphorically walk by a table of objects and you're going to see the most beautiful peacock feather and you're going to reach for it and then that voice inside you is going to slap your hand and say to you, "How dare you? Who do you think you are!" and you're going to recoil.

And then you're going to regret it.

Because something inside of you, something true and intuitive that was stamped on your soul the day you were created, knows what you love and knows what you want and sees such specific beauty in that peacock feather. But the voices of scarcity and shame and judgment—the Soul Bullies—were on the prowl, and wouldn't let you come alive in that moment.

Pick up the peacock feather, for crying out loud. In doing so, you are honoring the sacred space inside you that no one can get their hands on, no one can wreck. You are joining the song God already sings over you, and you are celebrating who you are becoming.

• • •

I believe I don't deserve . . .

But here's the truth . . .

day 94 THIS ONE'S FOR ALL OF US WHO HAVE LOST SOMETHING SACRED

I will make rivers flow on barren heights,
and springs within the valleys.
I will turn the desert into pools of water,
and the parched ground into springs.
—*Isaiah 41:18 NIV*

The last season has been the hardest of my life. I have found myself in the middle of my greatest fear, walking through the very situation I would have done anything to avoid.

My husband came home from back-to-back deployments—he had been gone the better part of a year—and told me he was pursuing divorce. While certain aspects of our marriage had been difficult, I was not prepared for this.

Despite my attempts to change his mind, he has remained resolute.

So this season has been about the dissolution of something sacred, something I had bet my life on. And there's no prescription for surviving that kind of loss.

As I write this, I'm looking out at the James River in central Virginia. From my desk, I can see the slow-moving murky water running parallel to me. It is flanked by lush green. About six weeks ago, the kids and I moved here from San Diego for the school year. We are here to be closer to my family, to slow way down, to get some space, to enjoy the changing seasons, to begin again.

It is hard and it is holy all at once.

Early on, God said to me: "You are not losing your person. You are finding your person. And your person is you."

Loss is reductive, by nature. In loss, we lose things. The great mystery is that losing is inextricably linked to finding. We lose, lose, lose, and in that loss we find what was underneath, at the center, all along.

I know so very many of you are in the midst of your own loss. Debilitating, life-altering loss. Loss of relationship. Loss of hope. Loss of identity. Loss of future. It feels radically consuming. Like me, you worry this loss will disqualify you, take you out of the game, render you incapable and unworthy. You're tempted to flag down the people in charge to let them know you can still play, you're not incapacitated, you still have what it takes, you're not irrevocably altered. You're tempted to hatch a plan, find the solution, fix it. And yet . . .

We catch a glimpse of a self that bears the image of God. A self that cannot be consumed by circumstances. A self that is absolutely loved. A self that is eternally held. No matter what. We find these things because of, not in spite of, the loss.

A voice is whispering to me as I watch the river . . . *Let it happen. Let it happen to you. The losing, the finding. The falling apart, the coming back together. All of it. Sit very still. Keep breathing. And let it happen.*

• • •

Are you facing an ending in your life? What have you lost? What have you found?

day 95 STOP APOLOGIZING

You do not have to walk on your knees for a hundred miles through the desert, repenting.

—Mary Oliver

Apologize when you have done something wrong, when you have made a mistake. But just for the record, the following are not wrong or a mistake:

Taking up space in the world
Being alive
Using oxygen
Having a body
Asking a question
Needing a nap
Living
Dreaming

I was looking at grapefruits the other day in the grocery store and someone came up next to me to look at grapefruits too. I immediately apologized—"Oh, I'm sorry"—assuming that my existence was in this person's way. I do this at the airport. At the post office. At the grocery store. When I'm working in the kitchen with someone.

I apologize for my personhood.

I took a hot yoga class the other evening with Tina and Erica and it was like therapy. Part of it was the heat, the movement, the candlelight in the corners of the room, but a big part of it was our teacher. She explained to us that our theme for the evening would be truthfulness, being truthful with our bodies, our limits. Throughout our practice she encouraged us to find our highest and best selves and to be truthful about what was "highest and best" for us that night. At one point in the class, when she was reminding us about our intention of truthfulness, she said, "Just to be clear, truthfulness is not the same thing as judgment."

Man, that got me.

Truth = I take up space in the world.

Judgment = I must apologize for the space I take up in the world because it's too much, too in-the-way, and too annoying to every other space-taker-upper in this world.

Truth = I have a body.

Judgment = I must apologize for my body and its particular maladies because if I don't, everyone will think I'm just fine with my body, which is obviously not possible or acceptable.

Truth = I need to breathe.

Judgment = I must apologize for the number of breathers I personally need because I am annoying the heck out of everyone with my out-of-breathness.

An apology is an admission that you have done something wrong, so the next time you are tempted to say "I'm sorry," be sure you're saying those words because you have made a mistake or hurt someone.

But whatever you do, do not utter the words "I'm sorry" because you believe you need to beg forgiveness for being alive.

You are allowed to look at grapefruits as long as you need to.

• • •

Do you apologize for yourself out of habit?

---

day 96 BRAZEN

> *"Here I am between my flock and my treasure," the boy thought. He had to choose between something he had become accustomed to and something he wanted to have.*
>
> *—Paulo Coelho*

The word *brazen* swam up from my soul and out of my mouth, intuitively, a few years ago. We were living in the desert of the Middle East, stationed there for my husband's job in the Navy.

At that time in my life, my interior landscape matched the Middle Eastern landscape: beige. The sky was beige. The sand was beige. The buildings were beige. This is how I felt on the inside too. A million miles away from home, taking care of babies in a foreign and volatile world, slightly traumatized and definitely hypervigilant from a massive move and the—hardly worth mentioning—civil infighting going on around us.

You have likely been through a season like this. Not the beige of the Middle East, of course, but a beige all your own—a season of infighting, a season of trauma, a season of displacement and disorientation. The light has become flat. A dimension seems to be missing. Breathing is about as much as can be accomplished in a day.

During those beige days, I saw something that woke me up for a second, in a subversive way. I was stopped on a dirt road near our villa. My eyes wandered out the window. Gutter water ran beside my car, and riding high on the tide were the most striking hot pink bougainvillea petals dancing along. I whispered audibly, like a murmur from beyond, "Brazen."

The dictionary definition of *brazen* is this perfect phrase: without shame.

In that dull sludge water, I saw my own longing reflected back to me, my longing to feel that beautiful pink instead of all the beige, all the sludgy gutter water. I wanted the color back. I wanted to feel freedom to do and be and dance and play. Freedom to roam and risk and create and work. Freedom to love and rest and taste and see. Freedom to make and believe and dream and fight. Freedom to speak up and speak out and to know what it is I want to say.

• • •

What is something that got your attention during a season of beige? Gave you perspective? Hope?

____

____

____

____

____

day 97 THE LONG WAY HOME

Sometimes you're not blocked; you're empty.

—Anne Lamott

When I was a kid, my brother Trey and I used to climb the neighbors' fence and pick pomegranates from their tree. My mom would let us eat the pomegranates as long as we put our bathing suits on and got in the bathtub to eat them. That way she could contain the dark, delicious juice.

On one of the routes back to our house today, I drive by a spindly pomegranate tree in the front yard of someone we don't know. At a certain time of year, the tree has red-wine ornaments dangling from its branches that seem far too spindly to hold such luscious fruit.

I slow the car way down in front of the house—like a total creeper. I take a picture of it and post it to Instagram.

"What are you doing, Mom?" the kids groan and moan from the backseat.

I tell them about me, the pomegranates, and the tub. And how their uncle Trey and I would sit in the tub and smear the magenta juice all over the sides of the tub and ourselves. We'd pucker our mouths if the seeds were too tart. And at some point the inside of our mouths would start to shrivel from all the acid.

My kids laugh at this. I find I'm salivating.

"Then Gran would come in and spray us down, and I'd watch the pink water swirl toward the drain."

"Can we go home already?" someone chimes in.

"Sure," I say.

And I put the car back in Drive and start heading down the hill and then up the hill toward our house.

The thing is—and I don't think my kids have caught on to this yet—that tree is on the stretch of road on the "long way" home. It's not the most efficient route into and out of our neighborhood. But I'm learning to listen to that voice inside me that's asking for doses of beauty, even if those hits are only found on the long way home, even if I have to drive out of my way to breathe.

• • •

What is one thing you need to drive out of your way to see?

____

____

____

day 98 WILL YOU LET ME HELP YOU?

If we can share our story with someone who responds with empathy and understanding, shame can't survive.

—Brené Brown

A few weeks ago my entire family had some form of the stomach flu. Lane and I had it the worst; we looked green for seven full days. This is one of my absolute least favorite ways of being sick, and the only thing that makes me feel better and helps me keep my sense of humor is remembering Emily's line from *The Devil Wears Prada*: "I'm just one stomach flu away from my goal weight."

At one point—while in the throes of this horrible bug—I was in the pickup line at Luke and Lane's school. Lane was in the car, throwing up into a bowl I had provided. And we were waiting for Luke, who was now recovered, to come out of class so we could scoop him up, race to Rite Aid for supplies, and get home before I threw up.

Another mom pulled up next to me in the pickup line and asked how we were all doing. I rolled my window down just as Lane threw up into her bowl. My friend heard the whole thing.

Here's the deal: Two times previously that same week I had caught this friend as she was taking her son into school and asked her if she could run one or both of my kids in as well. I just couldn't get out of the car. And she gladly did, as I would have done for her without a second thought.

So when she pulled up beside me and we both rolled our windows down to the sound of Lane throwing up, she looked at me and said, "What do you need?" And I deflected. I said, "Oh, we're OK. I'm just going to pick up Luke and run to Rite Aid to get some PediaSure and Pepto. It will be fine." (Lane wretches behind me.)

"Leeana," she said somewhat sternly, "I will go to Rite Aid and bring everything to your house."

"No, no, no," I said. This friend has a brood of her own and I knew it would be a lot for her to pull off an after-school errand with all of her littles in tow. Besides, I hadn't done any favors for her. We were newish friends. It would all be too much.

Then she leaned over her passenger seat and said to me slowly, "Leeana, will you let me help you?"

And all my protective edges turned liquid.

"Yes," I said. "Yes, I will let you help me." My shoulders dropped.

If I'm unwilling to let my friends in, let them see me in need, if I'm unwilling to create interdependence, then I will never experience the fullness of the relationship.

I don't know why I do this. Maybe I am intolerant of my own need, and I believe these friends will be too. Maybe I don't want to let them see how chaotic my life is, or feels, sometimes. Maybe I'm afraid of being burdensome and annoying.

If we're honest, I don't think any of us would say we feel particularly tolerant of our own neediness. In fact, if I'm honest, I have to confess I can be downright contemptuous of this naked part of me. How dare I need rescue? How dare I need saving? How dare I appear helpless? I buy into the lie that it's far more brazen to appear fixed, and so I must pack on a plastered periphery so no one sees the needy me. The needy me is unpredictable and inconvenient, I think. No one will like her.

We don't come out of hiding because of our competence and smooth exteriors—because we've finally got it all together. We come out of hiding because we learn to embrace, with compassion, all the varied nuances of our humanity.

Do not wait to let us see you until you feel you are ready—spit shined and coifed. These moments never come. Let us see you because you are not ready. And yet, you have listened to the compassionate voice of God speaking over you and within you and, with courage, you allow him to chip away at the plastered cast around your soul so that we may all get the unique gift of the fleshy you.

• • •

I need to ask for help with . . .

____

____

____

day 99 WELCOME IT ALL

The soul should always stand ajar.

—Emily Dickinson

I'm practicing the Welcoming Prayer today, a beautiful prayer that opens your hands and your heart and your body and your mind to the very thing you want to ignore, reject, repress. You literally welcome the feeling you want to avoid and ask God to help you sit with that feeling. The idea is that sitting with it, welcoming it in, helps reduce its power. Of course we always believe the opposite—that ignoring something will help it go away.

You literally welcome the feeling you want to avoid and ask God to help you sit with that feeling.

Haven't you noticed with things like longings, let's say, there's a persistence to the craving that usually won't just skulk off when told? We have to bring them closer instead of sending them away.

Father Thomas Keating, a Trappist monk who has dedicated his life to contemplative prayer, gives us these words for the Welcoming Prayer:

> Welcome, welcome, welcome. I welcome everything that comes to me today because I know it's for my healing. I welcome all thoughts, feelings, emotions, persons, situations, and conditions. I let go of my desire for power and control. I let go of my desire for affection, esteem, approval

and pleasure. I let go of my desire for survival and security. I let go of my desire to change any situation, condition, person or myself. I open to the love and presence of God and God's action within. Amen.[1]

After these few moments, I blow out the candle and stand up from my place on the floor and head back to other, equally sacred, practices like filling the Crock-Pot and folding the laundry and dealing with the junk mail.

Honoring my everyday skin and honoring my eternal soul, saying to all of it, "You're welcome."

• • •

Pray The Welcoming Prayer and then ask God what he wants you to welcome.

day 100 I'M COMING

And I'll be the poet who sings your glory—
and live what I sing every day.
—Psalm 61:8

At the end of Paulo Coelho's *The Alchemist*, the boy in the story is planning to return to his love. He has been on the pilgrimage of his Personal Legend. And he has found his treasure. In fact, he has found that his treasure was there all along, at home.

The wind picks up, the levanter wind blowing in from Africa. Carried on the wind is the scent of a familiar perfume, the perfume of the boy's love. And, also, a kiss that finds its way to his mouth.

Immediately the boy knows who has sent this scent, this kiss.

"I'm coming, Fatima," the boy says.

And the book ends.

I'm closing this book similarly. With the knowledge that we must fight like warriors for our treasure, we must seek out our voice and our desires and our space in this world, we must turn a listening ear to our longings and to God's voice, all the while knowing love was already there, always there, waiting for us to come home to it.

You were breathed into existence by God himself, and there is nothing anyone has done to you or anything you've done to yourself that can wreck it.

God has already anchored you in his love. You are already held. Through Christ, our freedom is secured, and we can rest in the grace that we are both complete and becoming. We are both: Free to rest. Free to run.

Some of the etymology of the word *already* is "from an earlier time." Yes, exactly.

The journey is less about arriving and more about returning: to the truth we already knew, to the love we already have, to the beauty we already see.

We are always being beckoned home.

Maybe "the treasure" is knowing who we are and where home is and who is waiting for us there. God looks for us in the quiet of the morning. He sends his love on the wind. He calls out to us, "Where are you?"

Our whole life is to be the answer, "I'm coming."

• • •

What are three truths you are taking with you from this book?

____

____

____

____

____

Acknowledgments

In a season full of transitions—many of them difficult—this book has been the right project at the right time for me. And I am grateful to those who believed in it from the beginning: my agency, The Christopher Ferebee Agency, my agent, Angela Scheff, and my editor, Andrea Doering. Pretty much anything that makes its way out into the world with my name on it is because of these three. They are angels, deeply loyal, and have stood beside me in the most meaningful ways.

Thank you to Angela for fifteen years of friendship and advocacy, for walking this long road with me, and for nudging me to keep going. Thank you to Andrea for believing in my work so entirely, for well-timed phone calls with affirmation, and for the most clarifying editorial guidance.

Thank you to the entire team at Revell, who continue to put their best into these books: Wendy Wetzel, Eileen Hanson, Patti Brinks, Kristin Adkinson and her team, and many more.

Thank you to these Warrior Sisters, fierce and beautiful and strong, who have surrounded me with such love, now more than ever: Ashley, Kara, Tatum, Jamie, Corrie, Tina, Linsey, Elaine, Debbie, Kate, Joanna, Wanida, Erica.

Thank you to the Millers, Hatfields, and Tankersleys, who brew coffee, sit in the school pickup line, wildly entertain kids, talk through ideas, PRAY . . . all so I can get my writing done. An embarrassment of riches.

Thank you to my kids, Luke, Lane, and Elle, who are the lights of my life. They are becoming the most amazing people, and it is the greatest privilege to watch.

As I put the very last finishing touches on this book, our community is saying goodbye to a dear friend. And so, I want the last words to be a tribute to the Hamilton family and a thank-you to Mr. Ken, who has shown us all how to live richly. May you rest in peace.

Notes

Day 19 New Life Starts in the Dark

1. Barbara Brown Taylor, *Learning to Walk in the Dark* (New York: HarperCollins, 2014), 129.

Day 21 Scared-Sacred

1. Parker Palmer, "A Life Lived Whole," *Yes!*, November 8, 2004, https://www.yesmagazine.org/issues/healing-resistance/a-life-lived-whole.

Day 30 Treating Ourselves as We Would a Dear Friend

1. https://www.etymonline.com/word/forgive#etymonline_v_11804.

Day 31 The Mystery of Transformation

1. Richard Rohr, "Change as a Catalyst for Transformation," Center for Action and Contemplation, June 30, 2016, https://cac.org/change-catalyst-transformation-2016-06-30/.
2. Richard Rohr, "Change as a Catalyst for Transformation," Center for Action and Contemplation, June 30, 2016, https://cac.org/change-catalyst-transformation-2016-06-30/.

Day 34 Threshold

1. Online Etymology Dictionary, s.v. "threshold," https://www.etymonline.com/word/threshold.
2. C. S. Lewis, *The Chronicles of Narnia: The Voyage of the Dawn Treader* (New York: HarperCollins, 1952).

Day 40 Who Is Holding Hope for You?

1. Richard Rohr, *Preparing for Christmas: Daily Devotions for Advent* (Cincinnati: Franciscan Media, 2012), 2–3.

Day 54 Why Am I Struggling If This Is What I've Always Wanted?

1. Aizita Magaña, "Waiting to Inhale: Why It Hurts to Hold Your Breath," *Science Creative Quarterly*, March 28, 2012, https://www.scq.ubc.ca/waiting-to-inhale-why-it-hurts-to-hold-your-breath/.

Day 59 Breathing Room

1. Henri Nouwen, *The Inner Voice of Love: A Journey through Anguish to Freedom* (New York: Image Books, 1999), 3.

Day 62 Borrowed Prayers

1. Carrie Fountain, "Summer Practice" in *Burn Lake* (New York: Penguin, 2010), 34.
2. e. e. cummings, "i thank You God for most this amazing," *100 Selected Poems* (New York: Grove Press, 1954), 114.

Day 66 Making Amends with Myself

1. Tian Dayton, *Emotional Sobriety: From Relationship Trauma to Resilience and Balance* (Deerfield Beach, FL: HCI, 2007), 2.

Day 92 Perfect Freedom

1. Henry Cloud, *Integrity: The Courage to Meet the Demands of Reality* (New York: HarperCollins, 2006), x.

Day 99 Welcome It All

1. Thomas Keating, *Open Mind, Open Heart* (Warwick, NY: Amity House, 1986).

Leeana Tankersley is the author of *Breathing Room*, *Brazen*, and *Begin Again*, and holds English degrees from Liberty University and West Virginia University. Leeana's writing has been featured in the *Huffington Post*, on CNN.com, and at (in)courage. She is a regular contributor to MOPS, as both a writer and a speaker. Leeana speaks to groups all over the country about waking up those beautiful and sacred parts of each of us that can go dormant. She and her three children live in Virginia. Learn more at www.leeanatankersley.com.

CONNECT WITH

Leeana Tankersley

at LeeanaTankersley.com

tankersleyleeana

lmtankersley

lmtankersley

- Share or mention the book on your social media platforms. Use the hashtag **#AlwaysWeBeginAgain**.
- Write a book review on your blog or on a retailer site.
- Pick up a copy for friends, family, or anyone who you think would enjoy and be challenged by its message!
- Share this message on Twitter, Facebook, or Instagram: **I loved #AlwaysWeBeginAgain by @lmtankersley // @RevellBooks**
- Recommend this book for your church, workplace, book club, or small group.
- Follow Revell on social media and tell us what you like.

 RevellBooks  RevellBooks  RevellBooks